SIKHISM vs SICKISM

SIKHISM vs SICKISM

BATTLES AND BETRAYALS

VAIDEHI TAMAN

White Falcon Publishing

www.whitefalconpublishing.com

Sikhism vs Sickism
Vaidehi Taman

www.whitefalconpublishing.com

For information contact:

(Shop No. 17 Hilton Society, Ram Nagar Road,
Borivali West, Mumbai, Maharashtra, India - 400 092)

www.vaidehitaman.com

Requests for permission should be addressed to
vaidehitaman@gmail.com

ISBN - 978-1-63640-538-4

Dedicated to

I dedicate this book to my Aai for her unconditional support, blessings and love for me in each of my endeavours.
I would also like to dedicate this book to my Afternoon Voice team. Without them, my journey is incomplete.

No creation in the world is a lone effort, neither is this book. I would like to thank all those people who associated with me during the writing of the book.

Vaidehi

TABLE OF CONTENTS

FOREWORD

What does Sikh History say?

The Sikh community has given supreme sacrifices for our Nation. These days a '56-inch chest' has become an over-hyped idiom, but if you look at the warrior history of Punjab you will realise what it means to have a 56-inch chest. The Independence war of the country had a trio known as 'Lal-Bal-Pal' Wherein the Lal stands for Lala Lajpat Rai of Punjab. In 1985, an event was announced in *The Free Press Journal* publication and the then President of India, Gyani Zail Singh had come to Mumbai to attend it. During that time, the President himself had made a phone call to the Shiv Sena supremo Balasaheb Thackeray and politely asked:

"Is it comfortable for you to come to the Raj Bhavan tomorrow morning?"

In reply Balasaheb humbly accepted the invite.

After hanging up the phone, Balasaheb was eager to know the purpose of the call by the President. But, as decided, Balasaheb reached the Governor House and Gyani Zail Singh welcomed him wholeheartedly. Balasaheb, in his typical style asked,

'Rashtrapati Ji, Hume Kyu Yaad Kiya?' (Mr President, why have you invited me?).

In reply, Gyani Zail Singh said, "Balasaheb, I wanted to Thank you so I invited you. After Indira Ji's assassination in Delhi, there were Anti-Sikh riots all over the nation. Hundreds of innocent Sikhs perished in the genocide. They were burnt alive, their properties were put on fire, but in Mumbai and Maharashtra, you saved the Sikhs. And made it a point that no harm was done to them." While saying so, Zail Singh had tears in his eyes. He expressed his gratitude and acknowledged Balasaheb's great support towards the Sikh community.

This is a fact, the entire nation had entered into violent activities against the Sikhs but in Mumbai and Maharashtra, they were protected. If Balasaheb had raised his finger there would have been a Massacre of Sikhs in Maharashtra as well, but Balasaheb had tremendous respect for Sikhs, they had sacrificed their lives for the Indian freedom struggle. Balasaheb worshipped Bhagat Singh, Sukhdev and Rajguru, the brave freedom fighters. On several occasions, Balasaheb had openly announced that some headless guards had killed Indira Ji, so why should the entire community suffer for this?

Balasaheb respected the Sikhs for their integrity to the Nation. During the partition of India, the number of Sikhs that were wounded were much more than the others.

They witnessed the breaking of Punjab; they have seen their dear ones killed and the division in their own family boundaries. In Punjab, it has been a continuous war of extinction of the Sikhs. In spite of all adversities, the Sikhs always stood for the soil of India. The Indian Army also has a majority of Sikhs.

History also tells us that the Sikh sword was actively used against the Moghul invaders. The state of Punjab which had Ranjit Singh, who fought against the bruisers to keep India free and independent, eventually got Bhindranwale who developed hostility against the nation. They found Pakistan and America closer to them. They tried to make the Holy place of the Golden Temple of Amritsar, the centre of Khalistan. But, at last, the Golden Temple premises saw the end of Bhindranwale during the reign of the Akali Takht.

But the ghost of Khalistan is yet to disappear from Punjab and Punjabis. Even today, if the Sikhs come forward in dissent, they are termed as Khalistanis, terrorists or extremists. Recently, when the Sikh community took part in the Farmer protest, the Bharatiya Janata Party announced that the Khalistanis were involved. But here is a question that BJP needs to answer, - "If Khalistan was involved, why did Mr Prime Minister surrender to them by repealing the farm laws? What was he scared of?" The BJP has done a lot of irreparable damage to the Punjab farmer's image. In Uttar Pradesh's Lakhimpur Kheri, a vehicle ploughed through protesters from behind which killed eight farmers. Can you imagine if Khalistan would have really been involved in the agitation, what would have happened?

Sikhs are self-esteemed, like the Marathas they have guts and are brave. Maharashtra and Punjab share a unique relationship. Sikhs have great respect for Chhatrapati Shivaji Maharaj and Maharashtra honours Maharaja Ranjit Singh. But, the letter that Chhatrapati Shivaji Maharaj had written to Moghul King Aurangzeb stating that religion should be for saving humanity and not for destroying it, often goes unnoticed. All the actions and reactions of Ranjit Singh was to unite the Hindu and Sikh community. In his kingdom, all religious representatives worked for the Monarch and that is how he could retaliate against the British. Even today the Sikhs fight for the Nation.

Maharashtra's great saint, Sant Namdev travelled to Punjab as part of his All-India tour. His preaching became a part of the 'Guru Granth Sahib'. According to Sikhism, there is only one Lord and 'Guru Granth Sahib' is their Sacred book. Bhindranwale and his Militia have become a thing of the past. Punjab has suffered never-healing wounds by extremists. Today, Sikhs in the country and abroad are doing a great job.

Without the vision of Dr Manmohan Singh, our Indian Economy would have gone into a duct. During the global recession, India suffered the least due to its economic reforms. We need to address the concerns of Punjab and the Sikh's. Accepting their efforts as well as their achievements and overlooking their worries would be a great mistake. In this aspect, Vaidehi Taman's book *Sikhism vs Sickism* seems to be very analytical and well-researched.

The real history of Sikhs, their sacrifice and bravery have been evaluated by Vaidehi Taman in a gutsy way. Freedom Fighter Veer Savarkar in his revolutionary work in Europe, after the Madan Lal Dhingra incident, ignored his ailment and wrote the History of Sikhs. In this, the history of the Sikh Kingdom from Guru Nanak Singh to Raja Ranjit Singh has been written. Before writing this book, Savarkar learnt 'Gurumukhi'. He studied literature from Aadigranth to Dashamgranth. He also studied the Historical novels of Cunningham and Prabhruti. The original copies of Savarkar's handwritten scriptures were either destroyed by the Britishers or the Britishers took them away so that they are not found by anyone. This is why the first Marathi novel about the History of Sikhs couldn't be published.

Vaidehi Taman's book in English gives a new vision to the Sikh history and the Sikh community. The sensitivity and strength of the Sikhs as well as their emotive opinions can be understood. This is not only the history of Sikhs but it is also India's history.

Congratulations, Vaidehi.

- Sanjay Raut
Executive Editor, Dainik Saamana

Vaidehi's book *Sikhism vs Sickism* is all about the noble Sikh religion and how some sinking entities try to project them as Khalistani whenever they voice their opinion or agitate for their rights. The book has one unique chapter on how VD Savarkar tried influencing the Sikh religion through establishing Hindu religious scriptures in The Guru Granth Sahib. The book also sheds light on the political betrayals and pre-independence battles.

The book is about the predicament of Sikhs across the Globe. It starts from the pre-independence era wherein thousands of Sikhs warriors had laid their lives for undivided India and fought against British rules. The partition of India was the division of British India in 1947 into two independent dominions, India and Pakistan. Post-independence, both Pakistan and the Congress party played Ping-Pong with Sikhs by indirectly luring them in the name of Khalistan. The Khalistan movement was the Sikh secessionist movement. Promoted as a separatist campaign, its goal has been to create a separate homeland for Sikhs by seceding the Indian Punjab from India to establish a sovereign, ethnoreligious Sikh state, called Khālistān ('Land of the Khalsa'), in the Punjab region.

The cynical agitated several times and the protests resulted in irretrievable violence. The 1984 Delhi Anti-Sikh riots caused the death of nearly 3,000 Sikhs after the assassination of Indira Gandhi, the then Prime Minister of India, on 31st October 1984, by her security guards at the gate. Almost 38 years later, most of its masterminds and perpetrators remain scot-free. On the other hand, all the Sikh youth who were then arrested on some pretext or the other have completed their punishments but are still languishing in jail. Most of them are now senior citizens.

After 75 years of independence, their struggle of preserving the Sikh cultural existence is still ongoing. Giving various references, the writer has also traversed through Savarkar's acceptance of Sikhs and Shiv Sena supremo Bal Thackeray's love-hate relationship with the community. He shielded them during most of the crucial period and also warned them when they created riot-like situation in Maharashtra, particularly in Mumbai. Above all the writer has expressed her worry over the virtual Khalistan movement groups that are poisoning young minds. The book also writes about Saint Bhindranwale's reform work and the continued fight for a separate Sikh state which owes its origin to the Punjabi Suba Movement. The Akali Dal – a Sikh-dominated political party – sought to create a separate Sikh Suba or Province.

For the Sikhs community, Bhindranwale is the most respected freedom fighter, saint and political combatant, whereas his extreme measures taken against established tags label him as an extremist. This political awkwardness has caused too much impairment to Sikh Commoners. This is all about the Battles of Betrayals of the Sikh community.

The writer has elaborated on the rising voices towards the release of Sikh prisoners and why the 1984 riots were not brought to any justice and furthermore. While protecting the rights of Sikhs as Indians, she condemns those sick people who presented horrible narratives about them.

Overall, the book has many historic references and quotes. She has expressed her worry for the Sikhs across the globe that are beleaguered by those with vested interest. Very precise in information and expression.

- Dr Bhalchandra Mungekar
Indian economist, educationist, social worker
and a Rajya Sabha member

Vaidehi Taman's book *Sikhism vs Sickism* is a soul-stirring trip into Indian history from the eyes of one of our country's oldest and noblest religions. The book dives deep into the entrenches of Sikh roots and draws parallels with some of the course changing decisions that the community made in history and in current times. The book explains how fighting for their rights comes naturally to this warrior community but how they have also been led astray, first by the British and then by the leaders who promised them a sovereign state of Khalistan. It is no news that the Sikhs bore the greatest brunt of the Indo-Pak partition. Their legacy created by freedom fighters like Lala Lajpat Rai, Bhagat Singh, Udham Singh and countless others was overshadowed by the killing of the then Prime Minister Indira Gandhi. This ghost of the past haunts them even today when they come together in dissent. The recent Farmers Protest is one such example. Even though they were protesting against the draconian farm laws, those in power termed them as Khalistanis and extremists.

The book manages to impress the reader with the thorough research and investigative journalism skills of the writer. From historical freedom fighter Veer Savarkar's keen interest in learning about Sikhism to Shiv Sena chief Balasaheb Thackeray's unflinching support for the Sikh commoners who were living in Maharashtra at the time of the assassination of Indira Gandhi. The book covers it all!

Vaidehi, in her unique style, draws parallels between the Marathas and the Sikhs. Both warrior communities have fought in great numbers against the Mughals and the British. The Hazur Sahib Gurudwara at Nanded, Maharashtra is the most revered by Sikhs after the Golden Temple. The teachings of Maharashtra's great saint Sant Namdev are also a part of the 'Guru Granth Sahib', the Holy scripture of the Sikhs and regarded by them as their eternal Guru. To encapsulate, Vaidehi's book is incisive and explores various touchpoints of Sikh history while making it completely relevant to current times. It gives us a unique perspective on the Indian history and hits the right emotional chords that will broaden your understanding of Sikhism and also make you feel proud of India's heritage and diversity.

My best wishes to Vaidehi for the success of this book, which it deserves!

- Narendra V Wable

Editor of Shivner & MMPS President

Not only in the country but everywhere in the world, Sikhs have made a separate existence for themselves. It will not be wrong to say that Sikhs are standing for those who have no one in the world. They were an ointment for the injured after the war, erasing the hunger of the hungry. The Sikhs have been serving all religions for thousands of years in the spirit of service.

When this book came into my hands, I felt that everything which should be considered about the Sikhs is in this book. I was very happy to read the book since it has been written after a lot of research. Although Sikhs are always taunted about being Khalistanis, but every coin has two sides and the same has been elaborated in this book. The incident of the then Prime Minister Indira Gandhi being shot by her guards on 31st October 1984 shook the whole country. After which around 3,000 Sikhs were killed in the 1984 anti-Sikh riots. It was a very sad incident.

On one hand, we talk about Bhindranwale and on the other hand, we are also compelled to think that the Indian Army has a majority of Sikhs within its ranks. Sikhs have made many sacrifices to save the country and even today, after listening to the stories of the Sikhs, their heads are filled with pride.

I don't need to write much about this book because if I write, I can fill many pages, but every page of the book is worth reading. Very good information has been churned out with a great effort. It is very special for the youth to read and understand *Sikhism vs Sickism*.

I congratulate Vaidehi. I am sure this book will be liked by people not only in India but also in the world.

- Dr Vipin Gaur
General Secretary Newspapers Association of India

PREFACE

My reason to write this book…
Sikhs had to deal with Battles of Betrayals…

The majority of Indian Sikhs don't want Khalistan. They don't want to separate from the Indian soil, they just want basic respect and acceptance. In this book, I have written how Sikh's have been politically betrayed in India. Some Sikh leaders had a lot of political ambitions though they were not fit for the party-political itinerary, while some other sections of Sikhs wanted to push the Khalistan agenda but that can never happen. Some issues are here to stay, not to be solved or resolved, the same as a separate Tamil Nadu, the Hindu Rashtra and Kashmir. These issues are political gasses; they are used for burning political agendas only during elections. With the mature voters such issues have lost their relevance. Go to Punjab and ask the average Punjabi or Sikh, if they really crave for Khalistan. Likewise, ask an average Hindu voter about Hindu Rashtra, they don't even know what Hindu Rashtra is all about. The Indian middle-class has routine challenges and their life goes by in dealing with them.

Those minute and rather insignificant number raising slogans can't be construed to be speaking for the whole community. The year 1984 was indeed a dark year for Sikhs as well as for India. It shouldn't be forgotten, and one must make sure that there is no repeat of such incidents. In recent times, the idea of Khalistan is being fuelled by some sections of NRI Sikhs who fled from the country a long time ago, and Pakistani ISI agents who want to disrupt the peace and harmony in India.

Sikhs demand basic respect from other communities. They have made several selfless sacrifices to shield others from cruelty, torture and death in the past and do so even at present. Their charitable work is enormous, they are known for helping people of India irrespective of caste, religion or creed. They are hurt when jokes are made on them and they are treated as entertainment entities. They don't want to be labelled as Khalistanis or extremists. A small vocal section sharing hashtags on social media, raising loud slogans or wielding kirpans do not represent the entire Sikh community.

That young generation of 1984 has now grown up and many of the older people have even departed from this world. The then young generation of Sikhs are now entrepreneurs, government employees, farmers and also part of the Army. The overall mistrust of the Indian state has been restored to utmost confidence in them. The injustice to the community still irks and spills out on social media. This is because of the Indian policy of going along with skirmishes against its own people. In the name of teaching them a lesson, murdering a bunch of them and denying justice to them recurrently. The riots are well-propagated plans to demoralise and break the minorities.

With time, the memories of this massacre may fade, but it will rank in Sikh History with the likes of the one orchestrated by Ahmad Shah Abdali, who also attacked the Golden Temple and massacred a large number of Sikhs. Punjab is a landlocked state, with two nuclear powers on both sides and the destabilised region of Kashmir to the North. There is no chance of being able to practice trade without aligning with either Pakistan or India. Punjab has no power sources or mineral resources of its own. The state's major assets are its rivers and the fertile lands. The rivers are blocked by the dams and water is distributed. Most Sikhs are not bothered with the idea of Khalistan but they are bothered by the idea of sharing their water and their resources.

The Congress party was solely accused for the 1984 Sikh riots; there were many congress leaders who were found participating in passing the orders. But to my surprise, ever since 1984, Punjab has been electing the Congress Party time and again, which means that the 1984 allegations against Congress hold no ground? Most of the Chief Ministers of Punjab were Sikhs and Congress loyalists, and the voters are also Sikhs. How is the anger against Congress translated into votes? Why are Sikh politicians supporting Congress? Punjab has endured the dark decade of the 1980s. The violence took a toll on both Hindu and Sikh communities. That is the reason the vast majority of Sikhs in Punjab do not want a separate homeland and a similar war-like situation.

The occasional shrill voices for Khalistan come from the NRIs in Canada and UK who have nothing to lose in India. They faced no brunt during the 1980s, nor do they have anything to lose if those dark days return to Punjab. Maybe these are some misguided youth who were born in the 1990s and who don't know what it was to live and grow up in the Punjab of the 1980s. The movement in the 1980s lost because Sikhs never identified themselves with the movement for a separate homeland. Mind you, even after Operation Bluestar many Sikh Generals in the Indian Army only resigned in protest, imagine what would have happened had they revolted? Their protest was against the Indian States and authorities and not against the country.

The Congress was always unfair to the Sikhs since the pre-independence era but the anger against them has almost faded in the struggle of choosing a lesser evil. Sikhs prefer to vote for secular political parties rather than trust communal politics. Punjab is mostly ruled by Congress. Captain Amarinder Singh, the former Chief Minister of Punjab, was once a scion of Patiala state and a former officer of the Indian Army. He was the first Indian parliamentarian who had resigned as a mark of protest after Operation Blue Star in Punjab. But later on, until early 2021, he was a Congress veteran and the CM of Punjab.

The decade-old Aam Aadmi Party (AAP) made its political debut from Punjab, and Sikhs across the globe were hopeful that this new party might deliver some justice to them by releasing political prisoners from jail. The Aam Aadmi Party turned out to be the biggest disappointment. Instead of sticking to its anti-corruption agenda, AAP got into unwanted politics. Now Punjab wants a peaceful governance and Congress has managed to do so. Above all, some political motivators were successful in creating a perception with the urban voters that AAP is being supported by fringe elements like Khalistani supporters. Some unfortunate events like the Sucha Singh Chhotepur event, also reinforced this belief. Chhotepur was the Punjab AAP convener and its biggest leader, but he was caught selling tickets. In India, being good and doing everything right doesn't guarantee you electoral success. Even those who considered AAP to be a reasonable alternative did not vote for the party in apprehension that the Akalis may return to power. Hence, those irritated with Akalis and supporters of AAP also voted for Congress.

Apart from political dilemmas and social stigmas, Indian Sikhs are still fighting for their religious and traditional identity. Why are they not allowed to disassociate from all other beliefs and adhere to Sikhism? Why do we try to establish their ancestry in Hinduism? Why is the Indian media also mostly biased against their faith? Why is their descent translated as Khalistan?

To some extent, the politically motivated media houses hardly have anything to offer when it comes to the minorities of India. Hindu supremacy is the prime agenda of mainstream media channels. Spewing venom against minorities, creating disturbing narratives about them is routine assignments for some sold-out media houses. And in this race the recent victims are the Sikh farmers; their protest was deduced as Pakistan-sponsored and a Khalistan sympathiser's event. There are many Sikhs who proudly serve India, they belong here and calling them terrorists is disgraceful.

During the farmer's agitation, one old farmer said on the allegation of extremism, मै अपने जमीर और जमीन दोनों से ईमानदार हु, कैसे यकीं दिला दू? (I am honest with both my conscience and my motherland; how can I make one believe?) The right to protest against the establishment is a fundamental right in a democracy and we all have equal rights in this democratic country. Thankfully, some parallel media houses were bold enough to echo the farmer's voice and gather support across the globe. These are the people who are holding democratic values against the authoritarian elements.

India's Sikh population stands at 20.8 million, which is 1.72 percent of the country's total population There is 1.7% of the Sikh population in India and they have been here since the late 15th century. Sikhism is the fourth major religion in the country. The Sikhs are present all over India and their contribution is equally huge in all the states' economy and welfare.

During the farmer's agitation, the headlines projected the Sikh farmers as Khalistani terrorists. One video showing a Sikh man threatening the Prime Minister Narendra Modi went viral and the entire agitation was branded as an anti-BJP protest. To counter this bias and menace, the agitating Sikhs came up with their own social media page called 'Kisan Ekta Morcha'. Facebook temporarily shut down that page. Then the Sikhs printed their news and circulated it amongst the farmers. The Kisan Ekta Morcha was the official update on the agitation, and it was restored in three hours following social media outrage.

Social media played an important role during the farmer's agitation. Initially, all kinds of media refused to show them and later they were peddling fake news to demoralise the farmers. Likewise, YouTube gave voice to the agitating farmers. The powerful use of social media and the strong will of farmers finally forced our PM to repeal the Farm Laws. Some see it as a political gimmick ahead of elections in crucial states. Some farmers are still agitating for a complete conclusion.

Till today, no media person was made accountable for making those derogatory statements and running those fake news. No media dared to talk. What has forced the Modi government to repeal those laws? Some media anchors were seen crying in their programmes, questioning Modi's soft approach, some went on to tom-tom how kind-hearted Modi is, but none of them were responsible for drawing accurate conclusions.

The Seva by Sikh's was translated as picnic, the voice of Sikhs was anticipated as the voice of Khalistan extremists, and the participation of Sikh women was fated as sold-out protesters. Film actors, media channels, anchors, IT cells and celebrities were unleashed against one community, and finally, most of the citizens started believing that the protesting Sikhs were terrorists.

This is not an isolated issue. Be it releasing political prisoners or Sikh agitators, media either remained mute or displayed their double standards. When Sadhvi Pragya was released from jail for health reasons, Congress leaders coined a term called "Hindu Terrorists". The entire media, social media, political leaders, Hindu religious preachers and sanyasis all took to prime-time debates with rabble-rousing media anchors by calling it 'Hindu-phobia'. Some went on to curse the fate of other minorities in India. I am not passing any judgement here, but if we feel bad to be coined as terrorists then why do the minorities in India have to be tagged arbitrarily?

Another issue that is agonizing Sikhs is the prolonged detention of Sikh political prisoners. This issue has grabbed global attention during recent times when a Sikh farmer of Haryana, Gurbaksh

Singh Khalsa, vowed to fast until death or release the prisoners who were not being released by the Indian State despite serving the minimum mandatory term of their sentences. But the Indian media was again mute and misleading. This issue was discussed on various global media platforms. We are a small newspaper, but our morality is way too big. Keeping calm on such crucial issues is a burden on my soul. I don't know how many people I will be able to reach but I am satisfied that I made the effort.

Maybe the non-violent, peaceful struggle of Gurbaksh Singh Khalsa was not dramatic enough to gain TRPs; maybe this topic is not commercially viable for them; or maybe there is no personal gain in this news telecast. After all media standards have unbeatable competition for advertisements. This is the reason Indian citizens remain unaware of the developments taking place in Punjab. They just know there was a threat to the PM's life due to a security breach; they just know how political scheming failed in a tug of war; they just know some female calling herself Sidhu's sister is washing the family's dirty linen in public; they know all that creates sensation but not sense.

Sikhs are not only political victims but they are sufferers in the entertainment industry too. Sikh jokes are another thing that Sikhs have to deal with every day. Many of us make merry with the jokes, ignoring and realising that it's just a mere joke. But, why do we make it a point of humour and that too not genuine humour? We make jokes on the appearance, communication skills and not so intelligent people. On the contrary, many Sikh personalities have been at the top in their respective fields.

When the whole country was divided into states on the basis of language, Punjab was an exception. Sikhs started supporting Akalis because they felt their culture and language was in danger. The mass protest irked Nehru and he made every possible effort to tame the Sikhs. Partap Singh Kairon, CM (congress 1960) worked hard for undivided Punjab and made it the most prosperous state. After Kairon's assassination and Nehru's death, the Akali leaders once again pushed their agenda for division of Punjab on a lingual basis.

Later on, Lal Bahadur Shastri took some good decisions and helped Punjab. In the meantime, one of the top congress leaders promised to give perks to Punjab if it got divided. This came true under the leadership of Indira Gandhi, who flipped all Shastri's decisions. Punjab was misused by the centre to gain votes. Hatred against them started rising in the country. In the early 80s, there was a conference in Amritsar where all the top Sikh leaders were called, but they felt discriminated against. The media was under the control of politicians so no news brought out the truth about all that was burning in Punjab.

Meanwhile, the Government started promoting *Deras*. Congress helped these *Deras* to open various new branches. This was done to weaken the Sikh agitation. Later on, the Badals also clandestinely supported the *Deras* to make Sikhs insecure. Time and again, the Sikhs were deceived and every time the opponents were different.

Non-Sikhs have often criticized Sikhism regarding their texts, ideology, and social traditions. But as per Sikhs and other philosophers these criticisms are faulty and prejudiced due to the poor understanding of the manuscripts, mainly the many dialects that have been used in these scriptures. They are also of the opinion that most of the western researchers who tried to interpret the eastern religious texts were missionaries who were biased and it did not matter whether they were translating the Quran, Vedas, Puranas or the Guru Granth Sahib.

Guru Nanak Dev was against ritualistic worship and exhilarated in the belief of one true God, which is the Waheguru. Western scholars have considered the worship and bowing as akin to idolisation worship, as observed by the Hindu faith, which in itself defeats Guru Nanak's ideology. Even though a few Sikh groups have put pressure on universities to include academic criticism of Sikh literature and history, but still the outlook towards Sikhism has hardly changed. They have to deal with various challenges from political linkage to protecting the Sikh cultural values Another intention to write this book was to report the aberration of Sikhism by the Sikhs themselves. Sikhism was coined by Guru Gobind Singh Ji. His main motive was to come out of the evil practices such as casteism, monarchy and social injustice. From an early age, Guru Nanak Dev Ji refused to wear the ceremonial "sacred" thread called a *Janeu* and instead said that he would wear the true name of God in his heart as a guard, since a thread which could be broken, soiled, burnt or lost could not offer any security at all. He never believed in following orthodox religious practices and created a new sect. His first words after his re-emergence were: "There is no Hindu, there is no Muslim". With this secular principle he began his crusade. He made four distinct journeys, in the four different directions, which are called Udasis, spanning many thousands of kilometres, preaching the message of *"Ek Onkar"*, that is one God.

These days Sikh leaders promote themselves as Dalits or upper caste or lower caste and dilute the very preachings and foundation of Sikhism. The politics of India has given shades and colours to this very poised sect. Similarly, when Dr BR Ambedkar gave *diksha* to Nav Buddha, The Neo Buddhist movement was religious as well as a socio-political movement among Dalits in India. It fundamentally re-interpreted Buddhism and created a new school of Buddhism called Navayana.

This religion rejected Hinduism, challenged the caste system in India and promoted the rights of the Dalit community. The movement also rejected the teachings of traditional Theravada, Mahayana and Vajrayana traditions of Buddhism, and took an oath to pursue a new form of engaged Buddhism as taught by Ambedkar, who told his people not to do human or idol worship, but look at the irony, they are doing both today. Many Navbuddhas even adhere to the Hindu religious practices such as going to temple, sporting threads in their necks and hands.

Guru Gobind Singh Ji wanted the Sikh sects to be pure to protect humanity and see God within them as One. The concept of oneness has really seen twists with changing political equations. All the ten Sikh Gurus clearly stated that they were human beings. They were simply blessed with the capacity to hear, channel and share the Sound of that Universal Teacher for others to hear.

They taught that no group of human beings was higher than any other group. They claimed that the common brotherhood and sisterhood of the human race was the highest reality. Their teachings empowered people to break the caste system, to overcome social habits that harmed women, to become economically self-sufficient, and to create a tolerant society based on the common humanity of all people.

We have witnessed many contradictions to these beliefs. I don't want to elaborate on it but just want to make a point that the deviation is sick. In Sikhism, there is no place for divisions based on caste. No Sikh is expected to consider himself superior to anybody else, for no man is born high or low. All are equal. A Sikh should be humble and modest and should have a desire to serve mankind. Guru Nanak does not divide men on the basis of their creeds. For him, men are of two kinds: Gurmukhs and Manmukhs. The former look to God and practice truth and work for the welfare of the entire mankind while the latter follow deceit, falsehood and selfishness. Whatever a man may call himself, he has to tread the path if he wants to attain liberation from pain and misery and from a mundane life. Everybody has to follow the same code of conduct.

The birth of Khalsa was a natural consequence and culmination of all that had happened before in the development of Sikhism.

Guru Nanak taught brotherly love for all human beings. He made it clear that man and the universe were indivisibly one. He guided his disciples to their own realisation and experience of absolute truth and helped them free themselves from the cycle of birth and death. This could be achieved without renunciation or practicing asceticism. He stressed that an individual could continue to act a part in the great divine play even while remaining in the stream of life; in fact, this was the ideal state to be in.

Punjab may not consist of hundred percent Sikhs, as there are many Punjabis who are not Sikhs, for example, Brahmins, Khatris, Muslims and Christians, along with the Jain and Aggarwal communities. A Sikh is a person who follows SIKHI (teaching) or Guru Nanak Dev Ji and the other Gurus and wears the five external identifications as given by Dasham Guru Gobind Singh Ji. Their *Kesh* (hair) is untrimmed or uncut hair (both facial and head), they wear an iron or steel bangle called *Kadha*, a *Kacha* (a long Bermuda type underpants), carry a *Kripan* (a small sword to be kept on their person at all times), *Kanga* (a comb to help maintain the hair and beard), and wear a turban. But these days many Sikhs have given up on this and conveniently adapt all contradictions.

There is a term called a 'Mona Sikh', a person who follows the Sikh of Guru Nanak Dev Ji and other Gurus but does not sport the external identifications. He mostly cuts his hair and shaves his beard regularly, because of reasons like health, hygiene or by choice and generally does not wear a turban. There are violent people, cunning politicians, selfish businessmen and women abusers in every clan and here is what the Sick side of Sikhism gets exposed to. There is a lot of inequality and prevalent caste politics in the Sikh community itself. I am not equating Sikh with Sick practices; I am emphasising that the Sickening practices by some of their own sects are dangerous to Sikhism.

Then Punjab chief minister Partap Singh Kairon.
Image Courtesy: Adesh Pratap Singh Kairon

Then PM Jawaharlal Nehru with then Punjab chief minister Partap Singh
Kairon in New Delhi on December 30, 1958.
The two leaders shared good chemistry.
Image Courtesy: Hindustan Times

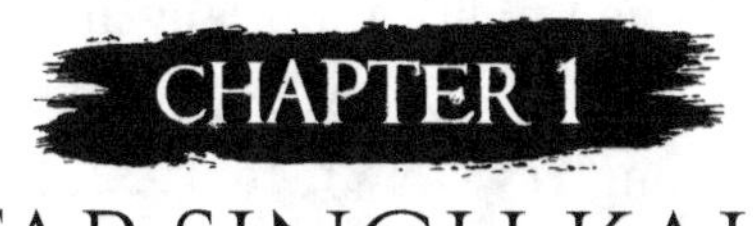

CHAPTER 1

PARTAP SINGH KAIRON
THE MAN BEHIND PUNJAB'S GROWTH

Partap Singh Kairon was the Chief Minister of Punjab domain and gave a huge face-lift to the state. He is regarded as the engineer of post-Independence undivided Punjab Province. It was later divided into Punjab, Haryana, and Himachal Pradesh. Kairon was jailed twice by the British as he agitated against the British rule. His political impact and views still dominate Punjab politics. His surname has been adopted from village Kairon in the Tehsil Tarn Taran of Amritsar in Punjab. His father, Nihal Singh Kairon (1863-1927), was a forerunner for commencing women's education in the state while his grandfather, Sardar Gulab Singh Dhillon, is famous for his farm reform works. His family have devoted their lives for pre- and post-independence Punjab.

Kairon was highly educated. He had gone to the United States to persue his post school education. From the University of Michigan he received his Master's degree in Political Science, while he did his second master's in Economics from the University of California at Berkeley. The farming methods practised in the USA left a deep impression on him and he wanted to implement the same in India.

After completing his education, he returned to India in 1929 and on 13 April 1932, he started a weekly paper in English, in Amritsar called *The New Era*. Ultimately, the newspaper was shut down as he joined politics. Initially, he became a member of the Shiromani Akali Dal (SAD), and after that joined the Indian National Congress (INC). In 1932, he was sent to jail for taking part in the Civil Disobedience Movement. He was the Akali nominee for the Punjab Legislative Assembly in 1937 and defeated the Congress contender Baba Gurdit Singh of Sarhali. He became the General Secretary of the Punjab Provincial Congress Committee from 1941 to 1946. The British Government jailed him a second time in 1942 for being involved in the Quit India Movement. But still in 1946 he was elected to the Constituent Assembly. In 1947, after Independence, he was part of the elected state government and held several offices which included Rehabilitation and Development Minister from 1947–1949 and later the Chief Minister from 21 January 1956 to 23 June 1964.

Initially, Partap Singh Kairon was elected as the Rehabilitation and Development Minister between 1947 and 1949. The Partition had displaced over 14 million people along religious lines, creating an overwhelming situation of refugee crisis. There was large-scale violence, migration and chaos, with loss of life, accompanying or preceding the Partition, varying between several hundred thousand and two million. This was an extremely challenging situation and as the Rehabilitation Minister, he had to settle millions of refugees who had migrated from West Punjab amidst tremendous confusion. Kairon is credited with re-establishing millions of refugees in East Punjab not only by providing them with new homes but also with job opportunities. In a very short period of time, he brought stability for them in the new professions with which they could support themselves and their families.

In 1952, Kairon was at the peak of his political career. He invited industrialists, such as the Oswals and the Jaijees, to invest in Punjab. The Partition had also cost the state its original capital—Lahore. It now needed a new capital. Renowned American Planner and Architect, Albert Mayer was tasked to design a new city called Chandigarh in 1949. During his tenure as the Chief Minister, Kairon helped in the creation of Chandigarh, which was completed in 1960. He also helped in establishing the industrial township of Faridabad, now the largest city in the state of Haryana and a major industrial hub. Punjab became the first state in India to have electricity in all its villages. The state's basic requirement of infrastructure in terms of irrigation, electrification and roads was fulfilled. Everything was going well until disaster struck.

In 1964, a lot of allegations were made against Kairon by his political opponents. Corruption charges were levelled against him. There were three probes; however, he was absolved of all three. A month after Prime Minister Jawaharlal Nehru's death in May 1964, Kairon resigned after being charged by the Das Commission. Nobody knew at that time that he was not only resigning from his post but also from his life. On 6 February 1965, he was on his way from Delhi to Chandigarh, when he approached Rasoi village in Sonipat district and someone shot him dead along with his personal assistant and driver.

The prime accused in the Kairon assassination case were Sucha Singh Bassi and his two associates, Baldev Singh and Nahar Singh "Fauji". Sucha Singh was convinced that Kairon had played a crucial role in the conviction of two culprits in a murder case, Ajit Singh and his father Bir Singh. They were in custody and under trial. Sucha Singh, who was closely connected to the convicts, believed that Kairon had taken a personal interest in securing the conviction of both the criminals. Sucha had deliberated the killing of Kairon in retaliation. All three conspirators, Sucha Bassi, Baldev Singh and Nahar Singh 'Fauji' were hanged till death in 1969 and the fourth Daya Singh, was given life imprisonment and was released in 1994.

Partap Singh Kairon had two sons and one daughter - Surinder Singh Kairon, Gurinder Singh Kairon and Sarbrinder Kairon Grewal, respectively. While the younger son, Gurinder remained a congressman like his father, Surinder later joined Shiromani Akali Dal. Surinder's son Adesh Partap Singh Kairon is married to the daughter of Prakash Singh Badal, Preneet Kaur and has been a minister in the then Shiromani Akali Dal ministry, but none of them made any noticeable contribution to Punjab like their father did.

Since Independence, many Indian National Congress (INC) leaders were killed for some reason or the other. These include Mohandas Gandhi, PM Indira Gandhi, PM Rajiv Gandhi, CM Beant Singh, CM Pratap Singh Kairon, CM Balwant Rai Mehta, CM Krishna Ballabh Sahay, Railway Minister Lalit Narayan Mishra, Legislator Vila Rati Ram Katyal, MP Lala Bhagwan Dass, MP Lalit Maken, MP Ragya Naik, MLA Vangaveeti Mohana Ranga, MLA Nand Kumar Patel, MLA Hardayal Singh and MLA Arjan Dass. In Punjab there were also a series of political murders of leaders of the Shiromani Akali Dal (SAD) which included MP Harchand Singh Longewal, Deputy CM Balwant Singh Thind, Punjab Planning Minister Malkiat Sidhu, Youth leader Vikramjit Middukhera, MLA Bachittar Singh and MP Jagdev Singh Khudian.

CHAPTER 2
SIKH NATIONALISM
ALWAYS RECEIVED WITH CONTEMPT

Sikhs are present all over the globe. They are rooted within their local and national communities, and remain loyal to the fundamental values of spiritual growth and social justice. Wherever they have habitats they establish Gurdwaras for their communities. Sikhs strive to maintain basic aspects of tradition within these contexts. They have been in the United States for centuries and have established themselves as active contributors to the civic society.

Thousands of efforts have been made to establish Sikhism's ancestry in Hinduism. No doubt that Both Sikhism and Hinduism have originated in India. Hinduism has been in existence since over thirty centuries, but was not formed until 800–200 BC. Sikhism, on the other hand, came into existence only around five centuries ago. Both have some marginal similarities. However, Sikhism has not originated from Hinduism. It is a distinct religion with different scriptures, social status, ways of worship, religious appearance, and lifestyle which is quite dissimilar from Hinduism.

Hundreds of blogs on the internet try to link the origin of Sikhism with Hinduism by citing some Hindu names of Guru Govind Singh, but those are just to prove how Sikhs have a Hindu origin. There is no authentic substance to prove their claims. Sikhism never forced conversions, they never forced people to adopt to get into their sects, rather it evolved ethically. They ask a non-Sikh to determine and live the vital message and meaning of their own religion so that a Hindu can become a better Hindu, a Dalit can be a good Dalit by following the principles of Dr Baba Saheb Ambedkar, a Christian can become a better Christian, a Muslim a better Muslim following the principles of Islam. Sikhism never dominated any religious principle. They always stood non-interfering, because Sikhs love their religion. Sikhism is equally respectful and accepting of other ways of life and beliefs.

Almost every religion, be it Christianity, Islam, Hinduism or Sikhism, they believe that a human is not only made of a physical body, but also has an individual soul. This individual soul is referred to as *"Atman"* or *Atma, Ruh,* Soul or *Rūha* in Punjabi. All these religions believe that the soul doesn't end with death but continues through the cycle of rebirths. This cycle can be broken by insight, which Hindus refer to it as *'Moksha'*, and Sikhs refer to as *'Mukti'*, Christians refer to it as 'Salvation' and Islam refers to it as *Nijat* (some call it *Bakhsish*). All these religions share the idea of *'Karma'*, that a person's actions in this life affects what happens to the individual's soul in a future life. This principle is similar to the English (Jews/Christians) 'You will reap what you sow'. These common concepts are shared by all religions in their own religious preachings, because these fundamentals somewhat match each religious base, but this cannot establish links to one another.

When it comes to the recognition of Sikhs, why do Indian establishments show limitations and treat such pronouncements as bravado? Clearly, they are aware that Sikh nationalism, even in an incipient form, poses a challenge to national unity and a commitment to secular political development. Punjab has a subtle geography, adjoining Pakistan just south of Kashmir, the Indian state long sought by Pakistan. There is widespread frustration among Sikhs who, though not ready to demand independence, say that they are hardworking and enterprising people who have contributed more to India than they have received.

Citing the same fear for the Prime Minister's life, the media went gaga over his security breach recently. Many media channels questioned Punjab government's intent to block the PM when Punjab's border is very closely attached to Pakistan. If we award that the state is on the border and some people are not happy with the status given to them, in spite of showing their love for India by shedding blood to secure her borders, why is there unwillingness to recognize them as a separate religion, as SIKHs? Why be obdurate by pulling them into the Hindu religious bracket? They are one of the minorities in India and they should be given their religious status just like all others. What Hinduism needs is to abolish the caste system, and invite everyone into one bracket. The dignity of humans is much more important than getting divided into Brahmans, Thakurs, Yadavs, Lingayats, Kayasthas and so on.

Some of the Sikh activists believe that the Sikhs were never betrayed at the time of partition. The British were willing to provide them with their homeland, but Nehru and Gandhi played foul with them. The Sikhs were told that they would have an equal share in the (post-independence) Government, but they lied. What they faced is Hindu colonialism, which threatened their survival. Sikh believers asserted their identity by never cutting their hair, by wearing a dagger and an iron *Kadha* and by using the name Singh, which means 'lion' and for females it is "Kaur".

Punjab has the richest farms and the highest per capita income. Sikh farmers produce the largest grain surplus. They are a sizable and prominent minority in Delhi. They are claimed as the most enterprising people. Many Sikhs are active in sports, politics, entertainment and entrepreneurship. They contribute hugely to the Indian economy. They contribute to the security of the Indian borders. There are dedicated Sikh regiments in the Indian Army. They are India's backbone in all respects, but still, they are fighting for their religious recognition.

The Indian Governments have never been fair to Punjab, knowing that it is rich in agriculture, the subsidies on fertilizers were removed. Sikh farmers are discouraged from selling grain at world prices and are coerced into selling at lower Government prices. But worst of all, the Government is impounding licenses from Punjab, depriving able Sikhs of openings in major industrial projects. They have farms, they have industries and even though they are a major part of the present Indian politics, they are still fighting for their cultural integrity. Thousands of Sikhs migrated to Canada declaring themselves political refugees. Sikhs are one of the largest minorities in Canada, US and other European countries.

Jarnail Singh Bhindranwale with an audience atop the Guru Nanak
Niwas in the Golden Temple Complex.
Image Courtesy: Sondeep Shankar

Self-styled general secretary of Khalistan, Balbir Singh Sandhu (right),
with a supporter showing Khalistani passport.
Image Courtesy: Sondeep Shankar

CHAPTER 3

SAINT BHINDRANWALE
DEMAND FOR AN AUTONOMOUS STATE

Master Tara Singh launched the Punjabi Suba Movement because during patrician crises, directions had been given to commissioners across the country to keep Sikhs under control and impose restrictions on them. Sardar Vallabh Bhai, the first chief of the three Armed Forces and Pandit Nehru accepted the condition of giving autonomous status to the state of Punjab. The Punjabi Suba Movement was a long-drawn political agitation, launched by the Sikhs. Master Tara Singh, however, was hesitant of accepting the measure, i.e., undivided Punjab was not ready to be part of either India or Pakistan. Pandit Nehru and Sardar Patel argued and explained to Tara Singh that the Sikh regiment was already a part of the Indian Government and it would be wrong if the Sikh regiment was in India and Punjab, on the other hand, would become a separate country.

Tara Singh was ardent in his desire to promote and protect the cause of Sikhism. This often put him at odds with the civil authorities and between 1930 and 1966 he was jailed on 14 occasions for civil disobedience. Early examples of his support for the Civil Disobedience Movement came through his close involvement with Mohandas K Gandhi. He became a leader of the Shiromani Akali Dal (SAD), a political party, which was a major force in Sikh politics. Singh's most significant cause was the creation of a distinct Punjabi-speaking state. He wanted to protect the integrity of Sikh religious and political traditions. In 1961, he began a hunger strike at the Golden Temple in Amritsar, promising to continue it to his death unless the then Prime Minister of India, Jawaharlal Nehru agreed to his demand for such a state.

Nehru argued that India was a secular country and the creation of a state based on religious distinction was inappropriate. Nonetheless, Nehru did promise to consider the issue. Singh abandoned his fast after 48 days. Singh's fellow Sikhs turned against him, believing that he had surrendered, and they put him on trial in a court ruled by *Pijaras*. Singh pleaded guilty to the charges laid against him and found his reputation in tatters. The community felt he had abandoned his ideals and replaced him in the SAD.

Meanwhile, the young Sikh was getting ready to live for the cause of Punjab. In 1965, Bhindranwale was enrolled by his father at the Damdami Taksal. Kartar Singh Khalsa, the religious head of the Taksal, died in a car accident on 16 August 1977. Before his death, Kartar Singh had appointed the then 31-year-old Bhindranwale as his successor. Bhindranwale came into prominence at a time when Sikh leaders were not much engaged with the community. He travelled from city to city, delegating, solving domestic disputes and showed no interest in a political career, seeing himself foremost as a man of religion. People started approaching him for addressing social grievances, and he began to hold Sabhas (Court) to settle disputes. Masses were happy to seek justice without the expensive, time-consuming administrative procedures that often did not ensure justice. Bhindranwale's verdicts were widely respected and helped him in gaining enormous popularity. Later on, he also appeared in religious text books.

In the 1960s, the Khalistan issue once again popped up when the autonomous status was officially not given to Punjab. The Akali Dal was created prior to independence to demand Khalistan to mark their political presence. The demands had been raised in both India and Pakistan. In 1966, Lal Bahadur Shastri died. Indira Gandhi's Congress party approached Bhindranwale in a bid to split the Sikh votes and weaken the Akali Dal, its chief rival in Punjab.

In the 1972 Punjab state elections, Akali Dal was defeated and Congress won the elections with absolute majority. In 1973, the Akali Dal put forward the Anandpur Sahib Resolution that demanded decentralisation of power and gave absolute authority to state governments. Somehow, the Congress put a pause on the demands but supported the candidates backed by Bhindranwale in the 1978 SGPC (Shiromani Gurdwara Prabandhak Committee) elections.

The Anandpur Sahib Resolution movement intensified, the Congress government saw some threat to their supremacy, and the demand for an autonomous state was forbidden. Jarnail Singh Bhindranwale then launched the Dharam Yudh Morcha in 1982 to implement the Anandpur Sahib Resolution.

When Indira Gandhi lost in the 1977 general elections, Bhindranwale had been recently appointed as head of the Damdami Taksal. Later, in 1980, Congress resumed power. Indira Gandhi and her son, Sanjay Gandhi realised that they could not manipulate Bhindranwale. At that time, the Congress CM (and later President of India) Giani Zail Singh, had supposedly funded the primary meetings of the separatist organisation, Dal Khalsa, amidst attempts to accommodate and capitalise on the outpourings of Sikh religious reforms in Punjab. Those days Sanjay Gandhi tried to lure Bhindranwale to support the Congress.

Following the electoral defeats of 1972 and 1980, tThe Akali Dal also adopted a similar electoral leaning. This resulted in a spinoff of the secular strategy. In the 1960s, Akali Dal aligned with Jan Sangh, an urban Hindu party. On hindsight, this was a blunder for the Congress, as it brought to fore Bhindranwale's political aims which gained popularity with the agricultural Jat Sikhs of Punjab, as he stood for the state's water rights, which were vital to the its economy, and also led Sikh reforms.

Bhindranwale pitched forty contenders against the Akali contestants in the SGPC elections in 1979, for 140 seats. He won four of them. A year later, with support from Giani Zail Singh, Bhindranwale selected candidates from three constituencies for the general elections. He won a number of of seats from Amritsar, Gurdaspur and Ferozepur. Though he had won but he did not seek any political office. He knew how to handle the Akali's and the Congress, both of whom had tried to exploit him.

Because of whatever association Bhindranwale had with Congress in those initial days, the ambiguous perception created was that Congress "created" Bhindranwale.

Bhindranwale's growing popularity and tremendous influence in vote politics created hazard for his life. By now the Congress and Akalis both realised his standing, and they started looking at him as a political threat. The Sikh community was very happy with this new found Messiah who was not only devoted to reforming the state and its people, but was also creating awareness by socially humanising people. Now the voters could not be bought by liquor or blue films. The young generation was prepared to speak for their rights.

Bhindranwale never respected the conservative SGPC or the Akali Dal functionaries as they had failed to support the Sikhs during the 1978 Sikh-Nirankari clashes due to pressure from their alliances. Neither did he surrender to the pressures of the leaders of the Akali Party nor could he be manipulated by the powers that be to serve their ends. He chose his own way to deal with such pressure tactics and also maintained his firm stand for the Sikhs.

During the Dharam Yudh Morcha, the Congress government used high-handed police methods on protesters as if they were hard-core criminals, creating state repression which affected a very large segment of Punjab's population. A tit-for-tat violence was witnessed from a section of the Sikh population, flaring the scope of the conflict by use of violence on its own people, creating fresh motives for the Sikh youth to turn to insurgency.

The idea of Khalisan was still ambiguous even though it was invigorated under the influence of Major General Shabeg Singh and retired Major General Mohinder Singh, former Sikh army officials who had been alienated by the government actions and had become consultants to Bhindranwale. This created unrest in the political corridors of Punjab. These two officers became the backbone of the movement though they were not directly involved. In other parts of Punjab, police and administrative atrocities created chaos. They subjected the common public to cruelty. This created irresistible anger and bitterness in the Sikhs against the establishment. Bhindranwale became even more popular amongst the influencers and Sikh intellects.

On the other hand, there was constant refusal and a sense of fear from Congress because of their highhandedness and the hopelessness of Akali Dal.

Hindu Punjabis took advantage of the situation by supporting Congress and the Sikh populace became the target. Sikhs are devoted to Gurdwaras as their faith centre. The section of these Punjabis living in Punjab created confusion in the masses, endorsing the state and central governments decisions. By 1983, the situation in Punjab was unstable. In October, the Sikh radicals stopped a bus and shot six Hindu passengers. On the same day, another group killed two officials on a train.

In 1974, the Congress-led Central Government dismissed the Punjab State Government (led by their party), appealing for President's rule. During the five months before Operation Blue

Star, from 1 January to 3 June 1984, almost 298 people were killed in violent incidents across Punjab. In the five days before the operation, another 48 people were killed in various violent incidents. According to government estimates, the number of civilians, police, and militants killed was 27 in 1981, 22 in 1982, and 99 in 1983. By June 1984, the total number of deaths was 410 in violent incidents and riots while 1,180 people were injured. Punjab became very violent and the Congress government was inactive during the law-and-order situation. Hardly any efforts were made to take this community in confidence and hear their voices.

In the meantime, saint Bhindranwale took shelter in the Golden Temple to avoid being arrested for the assassination of Nirankari Gurbachan Singh. He remained underground until the Home Minister, Zail Singh announced in Parliament that Bhindranwale had nothing to do with the said murder. (It is believed by some people that Bhindranwale had purposely chosen the Golden temple as he assumed that no one would enter or attack it. It was considered a safe place to keep weapons. Some are also of the opinion that Bhindranwale was a Sikh saint and to keep arms is the principle of religious belief but the Congress created a perception which suited them). The primary aim of the Congress was to eliminate Bhindranwale.

Operation Blue Star was launched on 1 June 1984. The aim was to remove Bhindranwale and his armed supporters from the Golden Temple complex. After a five days long struggle, on 6th June, they managed to assassinate Bhindranwale. The casualty for the Army was 83 dead and 249 injured. According to the official estimate presented by the Indian government, they apprehended 1592 and there were 493 combined military and civilian casualties. After this, the Indian paramilitary forces carried out various operations to clear separatists from Punjab.

The operation Blue Star and its aftermath outraged the Sikhs and increased support for the Khalisan Movement. The Sikh community felt a sense of insecurity and lived with fear for their life. The effect of this anger resulted in the assassination of Indira Gandhi, the then Prime Minister of India on 31 October 1984, by her Sikh bodyguards, Satwant Singh and Beant Singh. Gandhi's personal bodyguards critically shot one of the assassins.

while the other was convicted of her murder and then hanged till death. Public outcry over Gandhi's death led to the killings of Sikhs in the ensuing 1984 anti-Sikh riots. No one in power including Indira Gandhi, could have thought of such consequences.

A famous Novelist Khushwant Singh, a constant critic of Bhindranwale, had also acknowledged that "Bhindranwale's Amrit Prachar" was a resounding success. A number of reforms were taking place in those days. Most of the men swore in public to give-up liquor, tobacco and drugs and they were baptised into Sikhism. Travesties and business of blue films stopped. Men saved money that they earlier had wasted on addictions and alcohol, and started working lengthier hours on their farmlands, raising better crops. People in Punjab had become totally dependent on Bhindranwale and his killing shattered the Sikh community. They could not tolerate this loss. Each Sikh mourned his death.

Sikh shops and establishments were targeted and burnt in Delhi during the anti-Sikh riots in 1984.
Image Courtesy: AFP

The Sikh property was systematically identified and destroyed.
Image Courtesy: The Hindu

THE 1984 RIOTS

AT THE BEHEST OF POLITICIANS

The assassination of Prime Minister Indira Gandhi was in reprisal to her order to the Indian Army to attack the Harmandir Sahib complex in Amritsar, Punjab, in June 1984. The outbreak had caused in a lethal clash with armed Sikh groups who wanted greater rights and independence for Punjab. Globally, Sikhs criticised the army action and saw it as an attack on their religion.

Many films and documentaries have been made on these incidents. Many books were written on the Sikh Massacre that took place after the assassination of Indira Gandhi. During pre- and post-independence, the community had been betrayed by many political figures, this was another major treachery. The ruling Indian National Congress at that time, was actively involved in the riots. As per Government estimates, 2,800 Sikhs were killed in Delhi and 3,350 nationwide, while independent sources estimate the number of deaths at about 8,000–17,000 nationally.

In November 1984, thousands of Sikh girls and women were raped in front of their brothers, spouses and family members. Till today, no Sikh woman has got justice. During this period a lot of hatred was spread against the Sikhs in the country. Sikhs started reacting against the rapists, politicians, atrocious policemen and media persons. The situation was complex for them - political sabotage, social stigma of killing Indira Gandhi, no support and above all no place to go to. Mass killings and devastated families hardly had any strength to deal with the circumstances.

In 2011, the Human Rights Watch stated that the Government of India had "yet to charge those guilty for the mass murders". According to the 2011 WikiLeaks cable leaks, the United States mentioned the Indian National Congress's involvement in the riots and called it "opportunism" and "hatred" of Sikhs by the Congress Government. Even though the United States did not declare the riots as genocide, it did acknowledge that "grave human rights violations" had taken place. The Central Bureau of Investigation (CBI), the leading Indian investigative agency, also pointed out that the violence had been organised with the support of Delhi police and some Central Government officials.

In 1993, the Jain-Aggarwal Committee recommended registering a case against a local Congress leader, Dharam Dass Shastri. In 2005, the Nanavati Commission found "credible evidence" against Shastri, following which the Union Home Ministry ordered the CBI to reopen the case. But nothing happened, and Shastri is now no more. At the Karol Bagh police station Dharam Dass Shastri protested against the arrest of the Congressmen who were caught with property looted from Sikh homes. Brahm Yadav, the then Delhi Youth Congress president protested against a joint Army-Police raid in Kondapur, stating that the raid was conducted by a Sikh Army Officer assisted by another Sikh Police Officer.

The police with a strong-armed patrol would sit quietly in a corner and entertain themselves while a mob chased a group of Sikhs, including women, with sticks and iron rods. The police surrendered to the mob violence and fearing for their own life did not interfere. When the local police failed, Army units were brought in to control the situation, including a regiment of Soviet-made BMP Infantry Fighting Vehicles.

When the news was published in TV channels and radios about the Army's deployment, the mobs disappeared. They knew that this time they were not dealing with Delhi Police. The useless and inactive Delhi Police did a lot of damage to the common public's morale by becoming mute spectators. Those days many police officers went on leave.

For negligence during the riots, six Delhi police officers were sanctioned. The Supreme Court of India, in April 2013, rejected the appeal of three people who had challenged their life sentences. In the same month, the Karkardooma district court in Delhi convicted five people – Balwan Khokkar (former councillor), Mahender Yadav (former MLA), Kishan Khokkar, Girdhari Lal and Captain Bhagmal – for provoking a mob against Sikhs in Delhi Cantonment in November 1984. The court acquitted Congress leader Sajjan Kumar, which led to agitation and protests by the Sikhs.

One of the first high-profile convictions took place in December 2018 when the former Congress leader Sajjan Kumar was sentenced to life imprisonment by the Delhi High Court. This was based on re-opening the case by the Special Investigation Team (SIT) which was constituted by the NDA Government in 2015. There have been very few convictions in the pending cases of 1984. Death penalty was announced in only one case for the accused Yashpal. He was accused of murdering Sikhs in the Mahipalpur area of Delhi.

The judge argued that in the case of Sajjan Kumar, the witnesses were inconsistent - not naming him earlier, and only naming him before the Nanavati Commission set up in 2000. This argument was used again and again to acquit these high-profile politicians, but the logic given by the CBI ignores the active role played by the police in defending the powerful.

Three decades later also the police's silence continues. Chajju Ram, one of the constables on duty in those days told the court that Sajjan Kumar never addressed any gathering or visited the area around the police post. This is the same constable who says 'When I was on patrol duty, I did not notice any burnt house, or dead body'. Sajjan Kumar's acquittal was challenged in the High Court by the CBI, but those who claim to have seen him incite the mobs, have little faith left. The trial court found there was sufficient evidence in the Sultanpuri cases to frame charges against Sajjan Kumar for murder, abetment, rioting and spreading hatred.

Another Congress leader, Jagdish Tytler was always defending his innocence. The testimonies of two men who claimed to have seen Tytler incite the mobs during the riots have been rubbished by the CBI. Later, some Congress leaders successfully spread the rumour that the right-wing organisations took advantage of the situation by showing the Congress leaders in a bad light. Surinder Singh, the Head Granthi of Gurudwara Pul Bangash, in Central Delhi, is sure of seeing Tytler incite the mobs on 1 November 1984. The other, Jasbir Singh, claims to have seen Tytler at a hospital in North Delhi on the night of 3 November, asking a mob why only a few Sikhs had been killed in his area. In March 2009, the CBI cleared Tytler amidst protests from Sikhs and the opposition parties. On 7 April 2009, a Sikh Dainik Jagran reporter, Jarnail Singh threw his shoe at the Home Minister P Chidambaram to protest the clearing of Tytler and Sajjan Kumar. Because of the upcoming Lok Sabha elections at that time, Chidambaram did not press any charges.

The Nanavati Commission found the testimonies strong enough to say that "it is safe to record the finding that there is credible evidence against Jagdish Tytler to the effect that very probably he had a hand in organising attacks on Sikhs". But the CBI, which was handed the case, produced multiple witnesses to show that Jasbir Singh may have been lying. While Surinder Singh, the CBI says, "changed his statement multiple times".

By submitting the Doordarshan footage, Tytler claims that the entire morning of 1st November 1984, he was at the Teen Murti Bhavan, where Indira Gandhi's body was kept. Whereas the footage had no time codes. And the CBI never questioned the other VIPs who were present, on Tytler's actions. A former Joint Director of CBI, M Narayanan, who handled the Tytler case, admitted that the CBI may have come under pressure to not pursue the case against Tytler.

Then the opposition, Bharatiya Janata Party (BJP), had demanded an explanation in Parliament from the Minister of State for Personnel, Suresh Pachouri, who was in charge of the CBI. Pachouri, refused to make a statement. In December 2008, a two-member CBI team went to New York to record the statements of Jasbir Singh and Surinder Singh, the two eyewitnesses. Nearly, 500 protesters from various Sikh organisations throughout India, had gathered outside the court which was scheduled to hear the CBI's plea to close the case against Tytler.

Kamal Nath, another tall leader of Congress was accused by the Nanavati Commission for encouraging the rioters. In March 2012, Judge Robert W Sweet dismissed the complaint against Nath. The court lacked jurisdiction in the case. The 22-page order granted Nath's motion to be dismissed, because as per Sweet the Sikhs for Justice had failed to "serve the summons and its complaints to Nath in an appropriate and desired manner". On 3 September 2013, a federal court in New York issued a summons to Sonia Gandhi for her role in shielding the propagators of the riots. Later, on 11 July 2014, a US court dismissed the lawsuit against Gandhi.

April 2014 Cobrapost's sting operation stated that the Congress Government silenced the Delhi Police during the 1984 riots. They would broadcast messages directing the police to not act against the rioters, and fire brigades would not go to areas where cases of arson were being reported. In January 2018, the Supreme Court of India formed a three-member Special Investigation Team (SIT) of its own which was to probe the 186 cases related to the 1984 anti-Sikh riots. The SIT formed by the Supreme Court comprised of a former High Court Judge, a former IPS Officer whose rank was not less than or equivalent to an Inspector General and a serving IPS Officer.

In the Sikh annihilation, 442 rioters got convictions. Forty-nine accused were sentenced with life imprisonment, and over 10 years' imprisonment for three. In the first case of capital punishment in the 1984 anti-Sikh riots, death sentence was awarded to Yashpal Singh for murdering two persons - 24-year-old Hardev Singh and 26-year-old Avtar Singh, in the Mahipal Pur area of Delhi on 1 November 1984. Additional Sessions Judge Ajay Pandey pronounced this judgement on 20 November 2018, 34 years after the crime had been committed.

The second convict, Naresh Sehrawat, was awarded life imprisonment due to his failing health. The conviction had followed a complaint filed by the deceased Hardev Singh's elder brother Santokh Singh. They had filed an FIR on the day of the crime but nothing had happened because a Congress leader, JP Singh, who had led the mob, had been acquitted in this case. Following recommendations of the Ranganath Commission of inquiry, a fresh FIR was filed on 29 April 1993. The police closed the matter. The reason given by them was untraceable, despite witness testimonies of the deceased's four brothers.

The Special Investigation Team set by the BJP-led NDA Government reopened the case on 12 February 2015. The SIT accomplished its investigations in record time. Resulting the formation of the SIT, the first conviction of Naresh Sehrawat and Yashpal Singh came on 15 November 2018.

Akali Dal President Harcharan Singh Longowal, Indian Prime Minister Rajiv Gandhi, and Punjab Governor Arjun Singh meet at the Parliament House on 23 July 1985 to negotiate the Rajiv-Longowal Accord.
Image Courtesy: Hindustan Times/Virendra Prabhakar

Sant Harchand Singh Longowal (centre) at Takht Sri Keshgarh Sahib just days after signing the Rajiv-Longowal accord.
Image Courtesy: Tribune/Karam Singh

CHAPTER 5

PRESIDENT HARCHAND SINGH LONGOWAL
ASSENTATION

In the 1980s, President Harchand Singh Longowal was reinstated as the head of the Akali Dal. He pushed for a peace initiative that reiterated the importance of the Hindu-Sikh amity, condemning Sikh militants who were in favour of Khalistan. His role was to support the Akalis during the unproductive negotiations that were going on with Indira Gandhi. These unsatisfying outcomes weakened the public's faith in the peaceful dialogues with the Government. This, in turn, reinforced the extremists and separatists.

Longowal approached Jarnail Singh Bhindranwale to take up residence in the Golden Temple Complex at the Guru Nanak Niwas in December 1983. Later, he moved to the building next to the Akal Takht.

Meanwhile, the Sikhs in Punjab supported the insurgents through harsh police measures, harassment of innocent Sikh families along with arrests and fake encounters. People of Punjab were in a miserably ill-fated situation.

These brutal attacks on the Sikh community provided fresh motives for angry youth to join the rebels, who were declared

Martyrs by the community as they were killed by the Police. Sensing that the Police was biased towards Sikhs, the rebellious groups became highly vulnerable. A section of Sikhs turned to militancy in Punjab whereas, some Sikh militant groups aimed to create an independent state called Khalistan. Others demanded an autonomous state within India, based on the Anandpur Sahib Resolution.

Many Sikhs and Hindus who were not allied to any religion, endeavoured to establish peace between the Khalistan supporters and the Government of India. Akalis continued to witness radicalisation of Sikh politics, fearing disastrous consequences.

On 4 August 1982, the nonviolent campaign to attain justice from the Indian government began under the leadership of Harchand Singh Longowal and six other chosen members. These members included Parkash Singh Badal—the former Chief Minister of Punjab, Gurcharan Singh Tohra—President of the Shiromani Gurdwara Prabandhak Committee (SGPC), Jagdev Singh Talwandi, Surjit Singh Barnala—former Union Agriculture Minister, Sukhjinder Singh-former Punjab Minister, and Ravi Inder Singh-former Speaker of the Punjab Legislature. The campaign sustained for almost twenty-two months and over 2,00,000 demonstrators were in Amritsar.

Several individual demonstrations manifested during the campaign. There was an unexpected outcome of the protests. Longowal had declared that Sikhs would campaign against the injustices of the Central Government's at the opening of the Asian Games which were scheduled to begin in Delhi on 19 November 1982. To ward off any such attempt, Indira Gandhi approached the then Chief Minister of Haryana, Bhajan Lal, to stop the Sikhs travelling by road or rail from Punjab to Delhi, since they had to cross Haryana to reach Delhi. The Haryana police implemented this but it inconvenienced the civilians and army officials who were travelling for the ceremony. A mass blocking of traffic was done on major highways on 4 January 1983. On 17 June 1983, large-scale protests halted rail traffic. Article 25 (a) of the constitution which states that Sikhs are Hindus was publicly burnt on 26 January 1984. On 3 June 1984, Longowal declared they would call for civil disobedience by refusing to pay land revenue, water and electricity bills, and block the flow of grain out of Punjab.

To oppose the Central Government, the Sikh coalition held together till September 1983. This is when the frustrations of negotiating with the Prime Minister started taking its toll and it widened the gap between Jarnail Singh Bhindranwale and Jagdev Singh Talwandi for refusing to pay land revenue, water and electricity bills. Under the orders of the new Prime Minister, Rajiv Gandhi, in March 1985, the leadership of the Akali party were released from prisons. This was done to improve the situation and create conditions for negotiations with Sikhs. The Prime Minister's confidante Arjun Singh, who was the Governor of Punjab, also announced the relaxation of censorship on the Punjabi press, withdrew army control over certain districts, instituted a judicial enquiry into the November 1984 killings, lifted the ban on the All-India Sikh Students Federation and agreed to review the cases of thousands of Sikhs who had been imprisoned since the Army's had taken control of Punjab in the previous June.

Initially, 53 leaders were released. After a few days, Rajiv Gandhi addressed the economic issues of Punjab by announcing the establishment of a rail coach factory at Kapurthala, which would provide employment to about 20,000 people. On 23 July 1985, an eleven-point memorandum was signed between Harchand Singh Longowal and Prime Minister Rajeev Gandhi, after weeks of secret negotiations. This covered all the major issues which could not be resolved since the Alkalis had first presented their demands. This was opposed by several orthodox

Sikh leaders of Punjab and some politicians from Haryana Some of the promises could not be fulfilled because of differences of opinion.

Less than a month after signing the Punjab Accord, on 20 August 1985, Longowal was assassinated by the Sikh extremists who had opposed the accord. He was killed near the Gurdwara in village Sherpur, 90 km from Patiala. He was fired from a point-blank range by the assassin, Halwinder Singh. The bullets pierced Longowal's abdomen, resulting in his death.

During the early 90s when militancy had reached its peak in Punjab, the state was reeling under the terrible threat from homegrown hate with a considerable amount imported from across the border. The chain of events starting from Operation Bluestar to the 1984 killings of the Sikhs in Delhi and other parts of India, post Indira Gandhi's assassination, provided a fertile ground for extremist elements to flourish in Punjab.

Thousands of innocent youths were randomly picked from their homes on various suspicions, never to return, coupled with no answerability from the authorities. Many *"Amritdhaari"* Sikhs were taken as supporters of extremism and harassed at Police checkpoints on highways, railway stations and other public places, declaring them as anti-Indian agents because of their appearance and wearing the religious dagger. When there was overabundance of human rights violations against the Government and the Police for using excesses against Sikhs, the carnages minimised a bit.

Through 1987 to 1991, Punjab was under a not-so-successful President's rule and the state was governed from Delhi. Though elections were held in 1992 but there was poor voter turnout. The Congress (I), under the leadership of Indira Gandhi formed the government. They gave a free hand to KPS Gill, the Chief of Punjab Police. Under his command, a number of intelligence-based operations like Operation Black Thunder were launched which neutralised Sikh militants. During these operations the Police also killed a lot of high-value protestors and were thus, successful in suppressing the violence and put an end to the mass killings in Punjab. The last major incident of Punjab militancy was the assassination of Chief Minister Beant Singh, after which the insurgency tapered off by 1993.

On 31 August 1995, Beant Singh was assassinated in a bomb blast at the secretariat complex in Chandigarh. Seventeen others were also killed along with him which included three Indian commandos. Ranjodh Singh Mann was accompaning Beant Singh on the day he was assassinated. The suicide bomber was Dilawar Singh Babbar of Babbar Khalsa. The backup bomber, Balwant Singh Rajoana, was also convicted later. A Chandigarh court sentenced Rajoana to death in 2012. There were several protests against the decision and a number of campaigns were carried out to stop the execution of Balwant Singh Rajoana. On 28 March 2012, Punjab Chief Minister Parkash Singh Badal approached the then President of India, Pratibha Patil to seek clemency for Rajoana and the execution was stayed. On the request of CBI, on 7 January 2015, the Thai Police arrested Jagtar Singh alias Tara, the alleged mastermind of Beant Singh's assassination. Currently, Tara is in a Punjab jail undergoing trial though he has completed his mandatory sentence announced by the court.

First Chairman of the National Human Rights Commission and the 21st Chief Justice of India, Justice Ranganath Misra (was also known as the Ranganath Misra Commission).
Image Courtesy: Jansatta

Congress leader Sajjan Kumar leaves Patiala House court in New Delhi.
Image Courtesy: PTI

CHAPTER 6

CONSTITUTION OF SPECIAL INVESTIGATION TEAM

BY THE NDA GOVERNMENT IN 2015

Before the Special Investigation Team (SIT) constituted by the NDA Government in 2015, ten other commissions had been formed to investigate the riots and the reports that got buried in files without any action. The most recent, headed by Justice GT Nanavati, submitted its 185-page report to the Home Minister, Shivraj Patil on 9 February 2005. The report was tabled in Parliament on 8 August of that year. The commissions resulted in many of the accused being acquitted or never formally charged.

In the year 1984 November, Ved Marwah, Additional Commissioner of Police, was given the task of enquiring into the role played by the police during the riots of 1984. The Marwah Commission investigated intensely and tried most of the Delhi Police officers in Delhi High Court. Just when Marwah was completing his enquiries in mid-1985, he was abruptly asked by the Home Ministry to not continue further. The enquiries halted, drawing no conclusion.

In May 1985, the records of the Marwah commission were handed over to the Misra Commission. This was headed by

Justice Ranganath Misra, a judge of the Supreme Court of India. He submitted his report in August 1986, and the same were made public in February 1987. He stated in his report that it was not part of his terms of reference to identify any individual responsible for the riots and recommended the formation of three committees to do the needful.

On the recommendation of the Misra Commission the Kapur Mittal Committee was established in February 1987. It was also tasked to enquire into the role of the police during the 1984 riots, though the Marwah Commission had almost completed an enquiry in 1985 it was asked by the government to discontinue. The Kapur Mittal committee comprised Justice Dalip Kapur and Kusum Mittal, retired Secretary of Uttar Pradesh. The committee submitted its report in 1990, wherein 72 police officers were cited for conspiracy and gross negligence. Although the committee recommended the dismissal of 30 of these 72 officers, but not one has been punished till date. During the span of ten years, one after other commissions were formed, but none of them could establish any motive of the Delhi police or book any of the propagators. These enquiry commissions proved to be just eyewash.

On the recommendations of the Misra Commission, the second committee formed was the Jain Banerjee Committee for registration of cases. The committee comprised former Delhi High Court Judge ML Jain and retired Inspector General of Police AK Banerjee. The Misra Commission had stated in its report that no case had been registered, particularly those involving political leaders or police officers. The Jain-Banerjee Committee recommended the registration of cases against Sajjan Kumar in August 1987 but none was registered. In November 1987, a number of press reports criticised the government for not registering cases even though the committee had recommended the same. The following month, Brahmanand Gupta, an accused along with Sajjan Kumar, filed a writ petition in the Delhi High Court and obtained a stay of proceedings against the committee. This was not opposed by the Government. The Citizen's Justice Committee filed a writ petition to vacate the stay and the High Court abolished the committee in August 1989. The Citizen's Justice Committee filed an appeal in the Supreme Court of India.

Following the Jain Banerjee Committee, the Potti Rosha Committee was established in March 1990 by the VP Singh government. On the basis of affidavits submitted by victims of the violence, in August 1990, the committee recommended the filing of cases. Only one was registered against Sajjan Kumar. When a CBI team went to Sajjan's home, his supporters threatened them if they continued to pursue Kumar. So, when the committee's term expired in September 1990, they ended their enquiry.

Next appointment was the Jain Aggarwal Committee in December 1990 as a legacy to the Potti Rosha Committee. It comprised of Justice JD Jain and retired Uttar Pradesh Director General of Police DK Aggarwal. It recommended the registration of cases against HKL Bhagat, Sajjan Kumar, Dharamdas Shastri and Jagdish Tytler. Its suggestion was to establish two or three Special Investigation Teams (SITs) in the Delhi Police under a Deputy Commissioner, supervised by an Additional Commissioner, which would be answerable to the CID, and to review the work-load of the three special courts which had been set up to deal with the riot cases. The focus was the appointment of special prosecutors to deal with the cases. Like all the before mentioned committees, this too wound up in August 1993, and the police did not register the cases it recommended.

The third committee recommended by the Misra Commission was the Ahuja Committee, to determine the total number of deaths in Delhi during the 1984 riots. The committee submitted its report in August 1987, stating that 2,733 Sikhs had been killed.

The Dhillon Committee, which was headed by Gurdial Singh Dhillon, came into the scene in 1985. It was established to recommend measures for the rehabilitation of victims. The committee submitted its report by the end of the same year. Its major recommendation was that businesses with insurance coverage, whose claims had been denied, should receive compensation as per directions of the Government. Although the committee recommended that the (nationalised) insurance companies should be ordered to pay the compensation claims but since the government did not accept its recommendation, no claims were paid.

The Madan Lal Khurana-led BJP government appointed the Narula Committee in December 1993. Its recommendation was to convince the Central Government to impose approvals. Although Khurana took up the matter with the Central Government in the middle of 1994, but the Central Government decided that the matter did not fall within its purview and sent the case to the Lieutenant Governor of Delhi. The Narasimha Rao Government further delayed the case by two years by taking that much time to decide that the matter did not fall under its purview. The committee then submitted its report in January 1994, recommending the filing of cases against HKL Bhagat and Sajjan Kumar. Despite the delay by the Central Government, the CBI filed the charges in December 1994.

In 2000, the Nanavati Commission was established after dissatisfaction with all the previous reports. A unanimous resolution was passed in the Rajya Sabha for the appointment of the Nanavati Commission. This was headed by Justice GT Nanavati, a retired Judge of the Supreme Court of India. It submitted its report in February 2004, stating that recorded accounts of the victims and witnesses "show that local Congress leaders and workers had either incited or helped the mobs in attacking the Sikhs". The report also said that it found evidence against Jagdish Tytler "to the effect that probably he had a hand in organising attacks on the Sikhs". It also reported that a closer look was required in Sajjan Kumar's involvement in the rioting. The commission's report also absolved Rajiv Gandhi and other high-ranking Congress (I) party members of any involvement in the 1984 riots against the Sikhs.

The commission also reported that the Delhi Police had fired about 392 rounds of bullets, arrested approximately 372 persons, and "remained passive and did not protect the people" throughout the rioting. All this information is available on open sources for a good read, but so far no one has been held accountable. Commission after commission were designated for the enquiries, but the government has no will to act upon these reports as hardly any police officer has been prosecuted or punished. Even today, many Sikh families are yet to receive basic compensation and justice. Who should be blamed for this delay? Thankfully, the political equations have changed in Punjab. This time Punjab voters have shunted out Congress from power. It would be interesting to see how the AAP will make a difference to the lives of the victims as they are ruling in Delhi and Punjab, both crucial areas for Sikhs.

CHAPTER 7

SIKH POLITICAL PRISONERS
THE PROLONGED DETENTION

This issue grabbed global attention during recent times when a Sikh farmer of Haryana, Gurbaksh Singh Khalsa caused a cognizance among the Sikh circles across the globe. He vowed to fast until his death or to release the named prisoners who were still in jail despite serving the minimum mandatory terms of their sentences. But the Indian media was mute or misleading. This issue was discussed on various global media platforms. We are a small newspaper, but our morality is way too big and keeping calm on such crucial issues was a burden on my soul. I don't know how much I will be able to reach out to the people but I am satisfied that I made some effort.

Maybe the non-violent, peaceful struggle of Gurbaksh Singh Khalsa was not dramatic enough to gain TRPs for the media houses. Maybe this topic is not commercially viable for them; maybe there is no personal gain in this news telecast. Afterall, media standards have unbeatable competition for advertisements. This is the reason Indian citizens remain unaware of the developments taking place in Punjab. They just know there was a threat to the PM's life due to a security breach. They just know how political scheming failed in a tug of war. They just know some female calling herself Sidhu's sister is washing the family's dirty linen in public. They know all that creates a sensation but does not make sense.

The role of these media houses is especially of concern when two Sikh prisoners were released on parole and these so-called media houses were rabble rousing. There was prime time debate, there was national threat, there was baseless commentary and there was total unfairness. Before the parole in December 2021, Lal Singh, who had availed 20 parole releases, was termed a "terrorist" by certain sections of the lap media. Perhaps the only suitable reason to term him a terrorist was that he was convicted under the Terrorist and Disruptive Activities (TADA) Prevention Act for illegal possession of arms.

The media ignored the fact that Lal Singh had availed 20 peaceful paroles before the present one, whose jail conduct was good, whose police, village Panchayat, Deputy Commissioner and SDM's reports were positive and upheld his good conduct. There was no trace of any terror activity by him, and for possession of arms he had already faced jail term. The Punjab and Haryana High Court had declared twice that Lal Singh's case was fit for permanent release from prison.

Another prisoner, Gurmeet Singh coming out on parole was presented with endless conjecture. There were endless questions on his fasting to losing weight. Without any substantial medical claims there were media trials of him. Finally, doctors from Fortis Hospital got involved when the Punjab Government showed its concerns over the issue. Gurmeet Singh had been awarded life term in jail, but the Jail manuals also dictate that any case of a life term convict should be considered for permanent release after the concerned convict has completed 14 years in prison. This process is called Premature Release; and most common people are not aware of it. As per the various jail manuals in India, there are provisions for Premature Release of life term convicts.

The decision to grant Premature Release is taken by the executive (Government authorities) and thus, these are considered political decisions. But as the nature of decision is 'quasi-judicial', the Indian Supreme Court of India has laid down specific guidelines for the Government authorities to exercise this power. This year, three lawyers carried out a study on the pending jail petitions by convicts, criminal appeals in High Courts and remission pleas for Premature Release pending with the state governments. The court also directed the legal service committees to explore if the convicts who had undergone a substantial amount of their sentence are agreeable to withdraw their appeal from the High Courts and get released. This, however, will be voluntary and will not affect the prisoner's right to file an appeal, the bench clarified. Time and again, the Sikh Siyasat News has clarified issues pertaining to the Sikh community. Advocate Jaspal Singh Manjhpur, who has taken up these cases, also spoke to the media on several occasions to discuss the merits of these cases.

Another prisoner, Kishori Lal, a butcher by profession was sentenced to death in the cases related to the November 1984 massacre of the Sikhs. His death sentence was converted to life imprisonment by an Indian court. The Delhi Government recommended his Premature Release, though his crime was part of the wide-spread and systematic genocide targeting Sikhs throughout India in which thousands of Sikhs had been slaughtered ruthlessly. The media was again mute and no one questioned his release. Whereas, Lal Singh's case was a fit case for Premature Release but he is still languishing in jail. There are organisations which are making all out efforts to reach justice, but highlighting the issues correctly will help the citizens to understand what is actually going on in Punjab.

CHAPTER 8

DEMAND TO RELEASE PRISONERS

WHO HAVE COMPLETED THEIR LIFE SENTENCES

The year 1984 was a miserable period for the Sikh Community. They blamed the Congress Government and its leaders for trying to eliminate Sikhs but the very same people of Punjab voted for Congress and brought them to power. Even today, Congress is ruling the state and the Sikh genocide is fading from people's memories. The party that never did justice to the 1984 victims is ruling the state.

Now the country is supposedly free, but it is being run by those who have destroyed everything on religious lines. Any minority, whether it is Muslims, Christians or Sikhs are either traitors or unhappy and disgruntled for not obeying the Hindutva rules. Look at history! Sikhs were the first to fight for the country. Relatively more Sikhs died defending the Indian honour in the wars of 1962, 1965 and 1971.

The Colonel who took over the Chicken Neck area from Pakistan was a Sikh. He is still alive but lives without any show off. Two Generals, Gurbux Singh and Harbux Singh fought in the Khemkaran 1971 war and saved Punjab. Pakistani tanks are still kept in Khemkaran. History is evident of the fact that

Sikh's too have laid their lives for India and its freedom. Even today, many proud Army, Navy and Air Force Sikh officers are guarding the borders of the country. We all love our mother land and are equally loyal to India. Discrimination is politically motivated and gullible voters fall into their trap.

Prof Davinderpal Singh Bhullar

Sikhs are very supportive of the Aam Aadmi Party (AAP) when they launched themselves in Punjab. The Party had received huge donations from the Sikhs settled in foreign lands. The Aam Aadmi Party chief, Arvind Kejriwal, endorsed the release of the Sikh political prisoner, Prof Davinderpal Singh Bhullar, but now Kejriwal seems to have put the issue in cold storage. The irritated Sikh activists trended hashtag on twitter "#KejriwalReleaseBhullarNow". This time they have chosen the AAP Government with great hope. Let's see how Kejriawal and his party in Punjab and Delhi make efforts to bring home Bhullar.

By advocating the release of the Bathinda native and convict Davinderpal Singh Bhullar and supporting various Sikh issues, Arvind Kejriwal gave new wings to the political ambitions of Sikh hardliners. They whole-heartedly supported Kejriwal, hoping for the release of political prisoners. Malwa-based Sikh hardliners have already returned to the mainstream politics through the Aam Aadmi Party tickets.

United Sikh Movement (USM), a body founded by former Sikh hardliners, another Sikh radical leader in Malwa, Baljit Singh Daduwal, unified with Kejriwal and AAP to see the change that they expect. The former Khalistan supporters, including Bhai Mohkam Singh and Bhagwan Singh, a close friend of Jarnail Singh Bhindranwale, were also founders of USM. Besides, radical Sikh leader Baljit Singh Daduwal, known for his stiff opposition to the Dera Sacha Sauda, supported Kejriwal. The Sikh affairs wing of AAP has great responsibilities. The AAP win in Punjab was not on their merit, but it has been due to the extraordinary expectations.

After the Supreme Court of India vacated the 'status quo' order on 9 December 2020, advocate Jaspal Singh Manjhpur sent a representation to Arvind Kejriwal via email to issue the release of for Prof Davinderpal Singh Bhullar. The AAP rejected Bhullar's case for untimely release. After taking all the benefits from the Sikh community, the Aam Aadmi Party now maintained silence on this issue. So far, Arvind Kejriwal has taken no decision on Bhullar. But now, they got have got a whooping majority and can take the prisoners' issue on priority.

When Bhagwant Mann was announced as the CM face of the Aam Aadmi Party in Punjab elections, a TV84 journalist had questioned him about the "injustice" done by AAP by withholding Prof Bhullar's release. Bhagwant Mann said that the AAP Government in Delhi will take a decision 'as per the law'. He said that the file for the release of Prof Bhullar was with the L-G (Lieutenant Governor) of Delhi. Different Sikh groups have stopped questioning the Aam Aadmi Party candidates about Prof Davinderpal Singh Bhullar's release because they believe Kejriwal will deliver his promise. Rather, they served an ultimatum to the Aam Aadmi Party by demanding Bhullar's release.

Prof Davinderpal Singh Bhullar was a teacher at Guru Nanak Dev Polytechnic College in Ludhiana. In the early 1990s, he had absconded as the then Chandigarh SSP, Sumedh Saini, had picked up his father, uncle and friend who were subsequently harassed to death in police custody. Prof Bhullar tried to escape from India but was stopped by the German authorities during an air-travel stay on his way to the USA. German authorities did not realise the threat to his life that he was facing in India and he was deported back to the country in January 1996. He was arrested upon his arrival in Delhi.

A TADA court convicted him in a 1993 case and he was sentenced to death. Subsequently, the global Sikh community raised its voice against his death sentence. In March 2014, the Supreme Court of India changed his sentence to imprisonment for life. In June 2015, he was shifted from Tihar jail in Delhi to a prison in Amritsar. Due to his medical condition, Prof Bhullar remains hospitalised in Amritsar under the supervision of the jail staff.

In October 2019, the Union Government of India announced its decision to grant Premature Release to Bhullar. The Union Government had made this announcement on the eve of the 550th Parkash Gurpurab of Guru Nanak Ji. On 17 December 2019, the Supreme Court of India ordered 'status-quo' related to the matter of Prof Bhullar's release as the court had accepted to hear a petition moved by Maninder Bitta against Bhullar's release. The status-quo decision was lately vacated on 9 December 2021, as the Supreme Court dismissed Maninder Bitta's petition challenging Bhullar's release. When the Union of India has cleared Bhullar's release, why is the Aam Aadmi Party-led Delhi Government deliberately ignoring the matter?

The Union Government and Punjab State Government both have cleared Bhullar's release. However, as per law, the final orders of his Premature Release have to be issued by the State Government of Delhi as Prof Bhullar was convicted in a case pertaining to Delhi. Being the 'holding state', the State Government of Delhi can issue his final release order after taking notice of the Union Government and the State Government of Punjab's agreement in this matter. Advocate Jaspal Singh Manjhpur has made a fresh petition to issue the release order.

CHAPTER 9

SIKH PRISONERS LODGED IN JAILS

FOR THE LAST 24-30 YEARS

The Central Government announced the release of eight Sikh prisoners. Since then, there has been demand to release other prisoners who have completed their life sentences.

A five-member panel founded by Sarbat Khalsa Jathedar Jagtar Singh Hawara, claimed the release of the Sikh prisoners who have completed their life sentences. The panel released a list of 22 inmates lodged in different jails across the country, which included ten in Punjab jails and five in Chandigarh's Burrail Jail. Jagtar Singh Hawara had staged a protest in various places like Chandigarh, Amritsar, Nabha and Patiala demanding the release of these Sikh prisoners. Then the Punjab government had turned a blind eye on these demands. Punjab has given a chance to every political party that has ruled the state in anticipation that someone will help them in getting their people out of the jails, but the never-ending saga of betrayal continues.

Lal Singh was awarded life sentence in January 1997 for criminal treachery, under Sections of TADA, Explosive Substances Act and Sections of Arms Act. The explosives were recovered from his house. He belongs to Akalgarh village in

Phagwara and has been lodged at Patiala's Nabha high- security jail since 1992. He is soon going to be a senior citizen and all his life has been spent in jail, even though he has completed his term.

Gurdeep Singh Khera has been lodged in jail since December 1990. A life sentence was pronounced for him in December 2001 by a TADA court in Karnataka under Sections of murder, attempt to murder, criminal conspiracy and Sections of TADA and Sections of Explosive Substances Act. He is a resident of 'Jallupur Khera'.

Lakhwinder Singh alias Lakha of Patiala city, Gurmeet Singh alias Meeta of Guru Nanak Nagar in Patiala city and Shamsher Singh of 'Ukasi Jattan' village in Rajpura district of Patiala all were convicted in the Beant Singh murder case. These five convicts have completed their life term but are languishing in Burrail Model Jail Chandigarh since 1995. They were given life imprisonment in July 2007 in a case registered against them him in August 1995 for under Sections of murder, attempt to murder and criminal conspiracy and under Sections of Explosive Substances Act. Today, they all are in their early seventies. Paramjit Singh Bheora was also named in the same case and has been in jail since 1997. In the same case, Jagtar Singh alias Tara was also awarded life sentence in March 2018. Tara continued in custody in Burail Model Jail from 1995 to January 2004 till the Burail jail break. He was arrested again in 2015 and has since then been in jail.

Balwant Singh Rajoana has been in the Patiala Central Jail since 1995 and Jagtar Singh Hawara of Fatehgarh Sahib has been in jail from 1995 to 2004 till the Burail jail break. After his re-arrest in 2005, he has been lodged in Tihar Central Jail in Delhi. Though the Hawara committee had said that Hawara was neither a convict nor an under trial in Delhi, but he has still been kept in Tihar jail. The irony is that these cases are in cold storage, in spite of completing their term and having legal provision they are unable to come out due to lack of political will.

Subhegh Singh and Nand Singh both were conferred life sentences in a case registered in February 1995 under Sections of IPC including murder and criminal conspiracy. The Sikh community is facing bias from the judicial system and the governments that have had not allowed the Sikh prisoners to come out of jails even after they have completed their jail terms. That life imprisonment means till the death of the prisoner is clear, but different state governments have their own norms for premature release of prisoners who have completed 14-, 18- or 20-years' sentences with remissions.

The hunger strike in Haryana by Sikh activist Gurbaksh Singh Khalsa, who served a jail term himself on terror charges brought into prominence the matter of releasing Sikh prisoners. Most of these prisoners were arrested during the days of terrorism in Punjab and had been convicted for terror-related charges, along with intense politicking. These prisoners have served the mandatory time in jail and should be freed to lead normal lives. The Punjab Government has declared that none of the seven prisoners whose release Khalsa is seeking are convicts, while the ruling Shiromani Akali Dal has itself released a list of 13 prisoners where it wants the Centre's intervention since the Ministry of Home Affairs is authorised to recommend relief to the President. Gurbaksh Singh Khalsa's list of seven are part of the Akali Dal's list. Bharatiya Janata Party, the coalition partner, has reacted sharply to the demand for release. As per the national party president, Amit Shah stating that anyone connected with terrorism cannot be freed.

The Shiromani Gurdwara Prabandhak Committee (SGPC) has their own list of 120 Sikhs who are in various jails of the country despite having completed their prison term. It claims that of these, 96 Sikhs are lodged in the jails of Punjab. The government (through its Governors) can exercise other options in case they are willing to give some relief, at least till the final orders of the Supreme Court on the stayed remission process. In the light of the Apex Court's directions to the states, the Governors are vested with powers like pardon and suspension of sentence under Article 161 of the Constitution. Before 2007, a number of Sikh prisoners had been released on directions of the High Court, based on conditions like good conduct and state norms. One of these was Gian Singh, who was serving time in jail in connection with the killing of Sant Harchand Singh Longowal.

By writing this I am not advocating any terrorist to be released, but these are the fair demands of Sikh organisations because most of these prisoners were arrested by the Congress Government on grounds of suspicion. The BJP Government should once again assign an enquiry commission to probe the background of these Sikh prisoners and draw their own conclusion.

Through their lawyers, the Sikh community is trying their best to get relief for these prisoners, but political parties are indulging in empty blame games. Meanwhile, the Punjab Congress president, Pratap Singh Bajwa has lashed out at the Akali Dal, stating it was not serious about any issue. As per him, the Akalis have not done anything for those Sikh prisoners lodged in various jails of Punjab and elsewhere. Congress leaders, especially Captain Amarinder Singh, always remains calm by endorsing how happy the Punjab Sikhs are. The Punjab police has no answer why suddenly 13 Sikhs were arrested after the fast of Gurbaksh Singh? All this seems to be a game for the Akalis and Congress to divert people's attention from the drug issues. Sikh prisoners, atrocities on farmers, among all of it, the Aam Aadmi Party was the biggest disappointment. Even, SAD was least bothered about the release of Sikh prisoners. They all lack the political will to get these prisoners released, all of them are just worried about their vote banks.

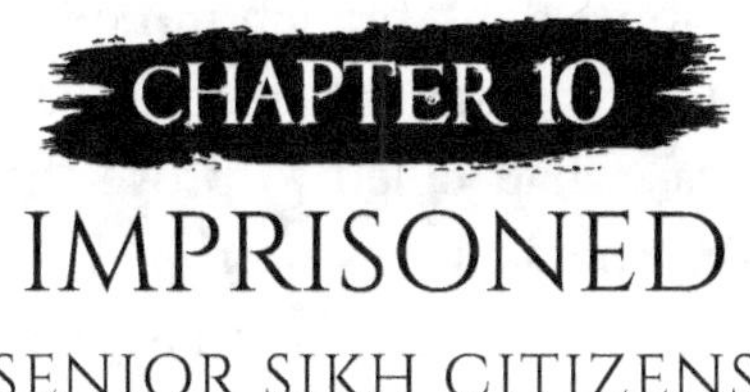

CHAPTER 10
IMPRISONED
SENIOR SIKH CITIZENS

The Shiromani Gurdwara Prabandhak Committee has made its own list of 120 Sikh prisoners who it wants to be released. They have approached various government and political leaders but most of them have debunked their appeal. Various Sikh organisations and some prominent lawyers like Jaspal Singh Manjhpur, have also come up with their own lists. Some have termed them these jailed Sikhs as "political prisoners". No doubt that Sikhs have contributed so much to the nation and the society. Several NGOs and Sikh organisations serve humanity without any discrimination. Person from any caste, colour or creed can take shelter and have Langar (Free meal) in any Gurudwara.

Organisations like Khalsa-Aid work for the betterment of the needy. Khalsa-Aid volunteers reach out to help during any disaster in the world. Pingalwara, Prabh-Asra, etc are some organisations that take care of the homeless and needy; they don't ask their religion before helping. But when it comes to their own demands and dissents the Sikhs are termed as terrorists or Khalistani separatists. While fighting for the release of political prisoners they are unable to convince the judiciary or lack in interpreting their stand and thus, the struggle goes on for years and years.

The Supreme Court acquitted nine persons who had been sentenced to ten years in jail under the Terrorist and Disruptive Activities (Prevention) (TADA) Act for looting Rs 5.7 crore from a Punjab National Bank branch in Ludhiana in 1987. This robbery was then the biggest bank theft in the country. The CBI, investigating the case, had failed to prove that the Rs 60 lakh recovered from the convicts was part of the looted money. on November 20, 2012, The TADA Special Judge, Ludhiana held guilty the Sikh Students Federation ex-president Daljit Singh Bittu and his associate Gursharan Singh Gama. Allegedly both of them were working with 'Gen' Labh Singh of the Khalistan Commando Force.

Bittu and his gang in police uniform, entered the Millarganj branch of the Punjab National Bank at 9.45 am and left with the money without firing a single shot. They had taken away old currency notes and had not touched the new ones valued at Rs 10 crore. This was stated by the then Chief Manager of the bank, SN Malhotra, in his complaint. The robbers had overpowered the guard and had threatened the bank employees and customers, who were made to sit on the floor. On completing 10 years in jail without bail, Bittu and Gama withdrew their appeal in the apex court. In 1987, eight men had been arrested for the unbelievable Rs 5.7-crore Ludhiana bank dacoity and all of them have come out on bail this year.

Maan Singh Dholewal (central jail, Ludhiana), Gurjant Singh and Harjinder Singh Lalli (Nabha jail) Harbhajan Singh, Saroop Singh, Balwinder Singh, Sewa Singh, Avtar Singh and Mohan Singh (model jail, Kapurthala). On November 20, 2012, these eight were sentenced to 10 years' rigorous imprisonment after a prolonged trial, by a TADA Court. The 70-year-old Maan Singh has undergone heart surgery and the 85-year-old Harbhajan Singh is not able to even walk properly. Now they are free men.

Even though there are many local news channels and newspapers in Punjab, but they hardly address local issues. Even the mainstream media is least bothered to look at Punjab unless some drastic tragedy happens. Let us start with Punjab Chief Minister Prakash Singh Badal, who held a special meeting with Bandi Singh Sangharsh Committee in the month of May 2015, which led to the struggle that was initiated by Bapu Surat Singh Khalsa, to sort out the issue of Sikh political prisoners. To decide about the pending cases against the Sikh political prisoners as per law, Badal set up a high-powered panel which comprised of an Additional Chief Secretary (Home), Chief Minister's Principal Secretary, Chief Secretary (Jails), Additional Director General (Intelligence and Jails) and four representatives of various Sikh organisations. The committee has been asked to investigate all the related cases to guarantee timely release of Sikh prisoners.

It is worth mentioning about the worsening health condition of Bapu Surat Singh, who has been on a hunger strike for the past two years for the release of all the Sikh prisoners who are lodged in various jails of India, despite completion of their term.

The Punjab cabinet has approved an amendment in the "Good Conduct Prisoners Act" of 1962, to simplify the procedure of granting parole to prisoners in various jails of the country. The thought was that after amending the Act in August 2015, it would be easier to grant parole to prisoners on the basis of their good conduct. However, the amendment has no mention about the Sikh political prisoners. The amendment has become a way to release political prisoners on parole.

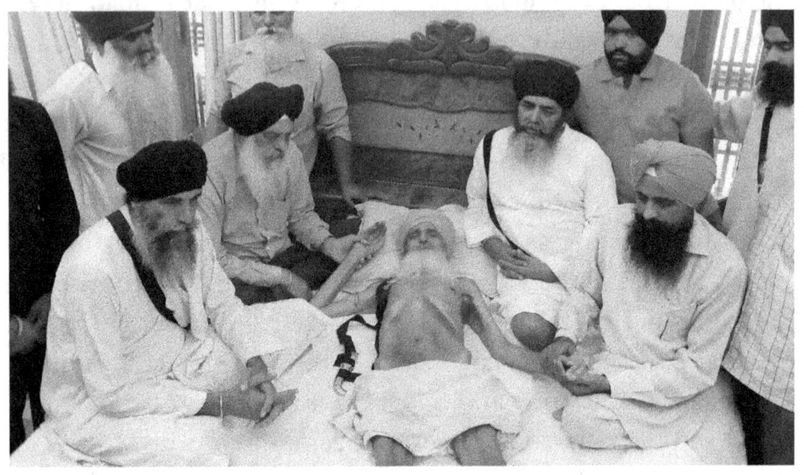

Bapu Surat Singh Khalsa while he was on the hunger strike.
Image Courtesy: Rubel Riat Photography

Bapu Surat Singh Khalsa wrote a letter to PM Narendra Modi in 2015,
informing him of his hunger strike to free Sikh political prisoners.

BAPU SURAT SINGH KHALSA
HUNGER STRIKE FOR BASIC HUMAN RIGHTS

An elderly Sikh man in Punjab shook the Indian Government by going on hunger strike for demanding basic human rights. He is asking the Indian Government to release the Sikh Political Prisoners who have served their term. From the 1970s Bapu Surat Singh Khalsa has been involved with human rights activism. He served as a guide during the Dharam Yudh Morcha, a political crusade launched by the Sikhs for equal rights in 1980s. He was government teacher who resigned his job in 1984 after Operation Bluestar. On-going with his advocacy for human rights, he became the secretary of the United Akali Dal (UAD) under the leadership of Baba Joginder Singh Rode, father of Sant Jarnail Singh Bhindranwale.

In February 1986, a police firing resulted in Surat Singh Khalsa being hit by a bullet in his legs. He has been detained in various jails, including Chandigarh, Nabha, Patiala and Amritsar in Punjab, as well as Kurukshetra, Rohtak and Ambala in Haryana during the 1980s. In 1988, he shifted to the US and became a Green Card holder. His five daughters and a son are also US citizens. He continued to remain active with Sikh political issues and was a frequent traveller to Punjab.

Surat Singh Khalsa decided to support those detained unconstitutionally after the Amb Sahib Morcha of November 2013 and the Lakhnaur Sahib Campaign in November 2014. During the first campaign for the release of Sikh political prisoners, Surat Singh Khalsa had declared that if anything happened to Bhai Gurbaksh Singh Khalsa, he himself would undertake an unlimited fast-onto-death until the Sikh political prisoners were released. When Gurbaksh Singh commenced his second hunger strike, Surat Singh Khalsa came to Punjab to stand in solidarity.

The Indian government was urged to evaluate the cases of political prisoners as a matter of urgency. He termed it as human rights violation. Bapu Surat Singh Khalsa refused food and water to seek the release of Sikh political prisoners who have completed their court sentences. On 11 February 2015, Surat Singh Khalsa wrote an open letter to the Prime Minister Narendra Modi, explaining the motive for his hunger strike. It is a question of unchallengeable rights of a person to live life without fetters. The question is about salvaging the liberty after one has completed the full term of one's sentence in prison. The question is about justice, equality and fair play. The question is about parity between the rich and famous and the poor and the underdog.

Surat Singh is a believer of non-violent protest. He also supported Anna Hazare's by remaining on hunger strike for several days. Surat Singh Khalsa always spoke against injustices to the Sikhs and other minorities living in India. He fasted for 200 days at a stretch, but no government paid any heed to him. There were numerous agitations for the release of these prisoners but no government in Punjab and Delhi has taken up this matter for consideration. Probably they are all fearful of losing the non-Sikh votes.

CHAPTER 12

YOUTH AKALI LEADER

JAGTAR SINGH BHAINI

Jagtar Singh Bhaini, a Youth Akali leader from Sri Anandpur Sahib put an end to his life by committing suicide. Jagtar Singh had differences with the SGPC member of his constituency and Education Minister cum MLA from Roop Nagar. There was a dispute over a piece of land, and the case was under trial in Court. Out of frustration, he jumped into the Bhakhra Canal. People found his moped and footwear near the Army Bridge on the Canal. It was very difficult for his family to believe that he could ever do this. The police also did not declare the incident as a suicide until the body was recovered.

Jagtar Singh was a close aid of the Damdami Taksal Chief Baba Harnam Singh Dhumma. Because of local political pressure, the police had allegedly framed him under a number of cases. He became helpless and that led him to depression. So far, there is no investigation nor is there any conclusion regarding his death. People have short memories and have also forgotten the incident. It has become an open and shut case.

Media is also clueless regarding this suicide. No one knows the background of his death. Suicide and drug addiction are major concerns in Punjab. The newly elected Aam Aadmi Party has declared that they would make Punjab a drug-free state.

The Sikh youth are a political and social victim. They are undergoing identity crises, rejection, allegations along with lack of opportunities. Drug syndicates from across borders have engrossed Punjab in their addiction. The Punjab youth are misguided from all fronts. A study conducted by Dr Ravinder Sandhu of Guru Nanak Dev University reveals that the incidence of such crimes in Punjab are nine times the national average. Between 1999 and 2008, the years when Punjab was recovering from the aftermath of terrorism, such crimes registered a staggering 245 percent increase. Punjab became the state with the highest number of narcotics-related crimes, surpassing Mizoram, which had earlier held this dubious distinction.

Mother Nature has also not been very kind to Punjab. The state is undergoing an ecological disaster because of agriculture supported by heavy use of chemicals and pesticides and overuse of groundwater. Thousands of acres of crops are burned to make room for the next season's crops, adding to a health crisis. Farmers are committing suicide due to overburden of loans and in such crises survival is a challenge.

No matter what these new WhatsApp historians want to make you believe, Punjab has always been an independent state. Punjab's fecund land has unmatched ability to produce legendary amounts of crops and ideals. The list of legends born in Punjab is ever-growing like its yields.

Since King Porus, Punjab has been home to Guru Nanak, and the following nine Sikh Gurus along with Baba Farid, Bulleh Shah, Maharaja Ranjit Singh, General Hari Singh Nalwa, General Zorawar Singh, Akali Foola Singh and many more exceptionally brave personalities.

Ever since the British consolidated the land and left it in the hands of two newly made countries called India and Pakistan, Punjab has been yearning for its former sovereignty and glory. To reinstate this status, Punjab is constantly at odds with the Indian Government. The struggle has gone from agitations and protests to armed fights.

CHAPTER 13

PUNJAB

WHY DOES IT ALWAYS BLEED?

Every battle by the Sikhs to retain Punjab for themselves as a sign of their territorial existence has been futile. Their contribution to pre-independence is equally huge. There are hundreds of historic evidences that the Sikhs were betrayed time and again. After partition, Punjab's border areas lost their population due to heavy migration to the country of their choice. If we look at the pre-independence Punjab region, Pakistan has kept it intact while India has divided its Punjab region into Indian Punjab, Haryana and Himachal Pradesh. At the time of independence in 1947, nearly all the Muslims from Indian Punjab, Haryana and Himachal Pradesh migrated to Pakistan or were killed in the riots.

At the same time most of the Hindus and Sikhs from Pakistani Punjab migrated to India or they too were killed in the riots. The population of Hindus and Sikhs in the Punjab region of Pakistan was less than 1%, while the Muslims in Indian Punjab, Haryana and Himachal Pradesh were double, mostly due to the migration of Indian Muslims from Uttar Pradesh and Bihar to these states. The partition of India was the outcome of the *divide et impera* policy of the Britishers which aimed to divide India on communal lines and rule as long as possible. Thus, when communalism reached its edge, partition was inevitable in which both sides saw communal riots and thousands of innocent people lost their lives.

Both countries had agreed that they would provide equal rights to all religious minorities. But Pakistan was created on the basis of a two-nation theory, wherein it was conceived as a separate nation for Muslims because they chose not to live with Hindus, who have distinct beliefs. So, Pakistan is not a secular nation, instead it is Islamic Republic of Pakistan and the rights envisaged for minorities are merely a delusion.

Punjab became defenceless against the violence and their so-called leaders could not keep their province united. There was drastic shift in their conduct as they were hurt and confused. Millions of Punjabi-Hindus, Muslims and Sikhs had been dismissed from the British Indian Army. Moreover, unlawful gangs were functional all over Punjab. Once the British had left, two partisan administrations came into power in the divided Punjab and random attacks on minorities started taking place.

At the end of the year, the number of racial cleansing was on the rise. Loss of lives was estimated between 500,000-800,000 and almost 10 million were forced to flee. After World War II, the first case of ethnic cleansing took place in Punjab. Therefore, it faced the brunt of the violence during partition. At the end of 1947, all traces of Muslim presence in the Indian East Punjab were wiped out, except for some Muslims who remained in the small state of Malerkotla.

Punjab partition brought a lot of dilemmas to Punjab. The partition created two hostile nations that have fought three wars against each other and show no signs of any meaningful discourse. The partition took place as part of reimbursement by the British between the Indian National Congress, the All-India Muslim League, and the Sikhs of Punjab to diving India and allocate power to India and Pakistan. At that time, the total population of undivided Punjab was 33 million. This included territories which were directly administered by the British and several important states. Punjab was a Muslim majority province while Hindus and Sikhs together made up a large minority of 44-47%. The principle for India's division was basis that the Muslim-majority areas would be separated India and be given to Pakistan.

Ishtiaq Ahmed's book, "The Punjab Bloodied, Partitioned and Cleansed", has chilling illustrations of human sufferings and the trauma of Punjab during separation. When the Muslim League demanded the partition of India, the Sikhs demanded that the same principle be applied to Punjab as well. The Indian National Congress (INC) wanted to keep India united but realising that the Muslim League was insistent on partition, on 8 March 1947, it threw its weight behind the Sikh demand for the partition of Punjab. Viceroy Mountbatten came to the conclusion that the partition of India had become unavoidable. Therefore, on 3 June 1947, the Partition Plan was announced which required the Punjab and Bengal assemblies to vote on whether they wanted to keep their provinces united or partitioned. Both assemblies voted in favour of partitioning their provinces.

The first comprehensive study of the partition of chronologically covers all the events which happened during 1947. Punjab consisting of 28 districts and all the princely states were under British rule from January 1st to 14th August 1947. As per Sir Evan Jenkins, the last British Governor of Punjab, approximately only 5,000 casualties had taken place till 4 August 1947. But from 15 August to 31 December 1947, these figures showed a staggering rise and were anything between 500,000 to 800,000 by the end of 1947. Sikh battles of existence and betrayals have a long saga that continues even now.

When there was militancy in Punjab, the reports repeatedly were that Zia ul Haq had promised to restore Lahore to the Sikhs as the capital of Khalistan. Later, it was claimed that there was also an agreement that Nankana Sahib would be in Khalistan, but would be given a Vatican-like status. Indian analysts had written volumes about this. According to them it was merely a clever bait-and-switch ploy by Zia, who was seen as extremely cunning and duplicitous.

Benazir Bhutto, who was then fighting against Zia, specifically called out in multiple interviews on why she opposed the idea of Khalistan. In an interview in 1986, the interviewer asked Benazir Bhutto, "In India there is apprehension that Pakistan is backing Sikh terrorists. What do you think of the Khalistan campaign?"

Bhutto replied "As I have said before, we stand for regional stability. We do not want any more break-ups in our subcontinent. How can I ever sympathise with the Khalistan demand? As you know, the capital of Khalistan is Lahore. The Khalistan map also includes half of Pakistan. I am not going to be party to further break-ups of Pakistan. My duty is to preserve the federation and not to break it".

Sikh militants who were being trained in Pakistan, more than once raised the Nishan Sahib banner on Pakistani soil because they assumed that they were on Khalistan soil. Reportedly, all this shocked Zia and he ordered that the militants being trained in Pakistan should be kept under strict observation because they could inevitably turn on Pakistan in future. Similarly, the growing dominance of Khalistani activists in Punjab were clutched by the Indian Congress.

Sikh separatists often maintained in their interviews that Pakistan had promised them that Lahore would be handed over to them once Khalistan came into existence. Some even suggested a trade to Pakistan. They would give them Kashmir and take all of Punjab and relocate some of the Muslims. In Kashmir, Khalistanis had a limited role to play and they could not fulfil their ambitions due to constant military surveillances.

Sikhs are the ones who attacked Afghanistan and severed, what is today called Khyber Pakhtunkhwa, from it. Afghanistan has never accepted these as part of Pakistan. Most of the maps of the proposed Khalistan included varying parts of Pakistan. It has been more than 75 years of Independence but the Khalistan dream will never be fulfilled. No matter what, India is not ready for another partition and Pakistan would not lose one of their most prosperous states.

The struggle of the Sikhs had started much before Independence. As the British Empire began to perish in the 1930s, Sikhs had made their first call for a Sikh native land. When the Lahore Resolution of the Muslim League demanded that Punjab be made into a Muslim state, the Akalis viewed it as an attempt to seize a historically Sikh territory. Before the 1947 partition of India, Sikhs were not in majority in any of the districts of the pre-partition British Punjab Province, other than Ludhiana, where Sikhs formed 41.6% of the population. Rather, districts in the region had a majority of either the Hindus or the Muslims depending on its location in the province.

This territorialisation of the Sikh community was supposed to be formalised in March 1946, when the Sikh political party, Akali Dal, passed a resolution proclaiming the natural association of Punjab and the Sikh religious community. Despite having its first phase in the early 20th century, Khalistan as a separatist movement was never a major issue until the late 1970s and 1980s when it began to militarise.

There are two separate tales about the origin of the call for a sovereign Khalistan. One refers to the events within India, while the other refers to the role of the Sikh movement. Even the precise geographical borders of the proposed state differ, although it was generally imagined to be carved out from one of the various historical constructions of Punjab.

Established on 14 December 1920, the Shiromani Akali Dal was a Sikh political party that sought to form a government in

Punjab. Following the partition of the Punjabi Suba Movement, led by Akali Dal, it sought the creation of a province (suba) for the Punjabi people. The Akali Dal's maximal position of demands was a sovereign state (Khalistan), while its minimal position was to have an autonomous state within India. The issues raised during the Punjabi Suba Movement were later used as a premise for the creation of a separate Sikh country by advocates of Khalistan. As the religion-based partition of India had led to much bloodshed, the Indian government initially rejected the demand, concerned that creating a Punjabi-majority state would effectively mean yet again creating a state based on religious grounds.

The process of Sikh isolation from the national mainstream was set into motion shortly after Independence due to the communalism of national and regional parties. Later, the organisation was aggravated by the Congress mishandling the local politicians and other factions. Many observers believe that the separatist sentiments began in 1951 when Punjabi Hindus disowned the Punjabi language under the influence of radical elements. This created mutual suspicion, bitterness, and further misunderstanding between the two communities. The 1966 unresolved status of Chandigarh and the distribution of river waters intensified these bitter feelings.

While the Green Revolution in Punjab had several positive impacts, the introduction of mechanised agricultural techniques led to uneven distribution of wealth. The industrial development did not happen at the same pace as the agricultural development took place. The Indian Government had been reluctant to set up heavy industries in Punjab due to its status as a high-risk border state with Pakistan. The resulting unemployed rural Sikh youth were drawn to the militant groups, or pushed towards drugs and dope so they could focus less on the political injustice. Even the Government failed to address these crucial issues to safeguard the future of the Punjabi youth. Many films have been made on the Punjab youth being drawn into drugs, but the movie "Udta Punjab" has shown this beautifully. Due to drug addiction, cases of crime, rape, molestation and robbery have gone up. Most privileged Punjabi's have started quitting India.

In 1973, the Akali Dal had put forward the Anandpur Sahib Resolution to address the people's grievances by demanding more sovereignty to Punjab. The resolution included both religious and political issues. It asked for recognising Sikhism as a religion. The Resolution was rejected by the then Congress Government as a secessionist document. Thousands of people joined the movement, believing it as a real solution to the demands of a larger share of water for irrigation and the return of Chandigarh to Punjab.

In 1978, the Sikhs and Nirankaris jarred within the Sikh community. But the pro-Sant Nirankari stance of some Hindus in Punjab and Delhi led to further division, including the Jan Sangh members like Harbans Lal Khanna joining the fray. In a protest against the Holy city status for Amritsar, Khanna raised provocative slogans like "Kachha, karha, kirpan, bhejo inko Pakistan" ("those who wear the 5 Ks (Sikhs), send them to Pakistan"), which led to aggressive counter demonstrations.

Bhindranwale shot to prominence in the Sikh political circle by his policy of getting the Anandpur Sahib Resolution passed. Indira Gandhi rejected the Resolution. The Government was of the view that passing of the resolution would have allowed Punjab to be independent.

Punjabi Sikhs took to the roads by taking part in the Dharam Yudh Morcha. To control the Morcha, Congress deployed the police, giving them a free hand to deal with the protestors. High-handed police methods which are normally used on common criminals were used on these protesters. A very large segment of Punjab's population reciprocated the violence of the cops with violence. This flared the conflict by the state using violence against its own people. This created fresh motives for the Sikh youth to turn to rebellion.

Creating Khalistan as another nation like Pakistan was unclear and at that point, this issue was not connected to the movement headed then. In some parts of Punjab, a state of chaos and repressive police methods together brought about anger in the Sikh masses which was directed against the authorities. Extrajudicial slaughters by the police of Sikh youth in the rural areas of Punjab, during 1982 and early 1983, incited further reprisals. Over 190 Sikhs were killed during the first 19 months of the protest.

Nirankaris, Hindus and even 39 Sikhs opposed to Bhindranwale were killed. The total number of deaths were 410 and 1,180 people were injured.

Shabeg Singh, Balbir Singh and Amrik Singh, these three prominent Sikhs were shot in that operation. It was alleged that these three members had visited Pakistan multiple times between the years 1981 and 1983. Intelligence Bureau had reported that the Gurudwaras in Jammu & Kashmir and Himachal Pradesh were providing weapons training. The Soviet intelligence agency KGB tipped off the Indian agency RAW about CIA and ISI working together on a plan with a code name "Gibraltar".

A clean-up operation called "Operation Woodrose" was initiated all over Punjab. From the heavily enclosed Akal Takht, tanks and heavy weaponry were used against the militants. Anti-tank and machine-gun fire was also used. After a 24-hour long attack, the army gained control of the temple complex. The figures for the Army registered 83 dead and 249 injured. The militants attributed high civilian casualties as they had used pilgrims trapped inside the temple as human shields. After this savagery, Sikhs were very much at unrest.

The Battle of Ferozeshah was fought on 21 December and 22 December 1845 between the British East India Company and the Sikh Empire. Art by H Martens/Wikimedia Commons

14th Light Dragoons charging at the Battle of Ramnagar on 22nd November 1848 during the Second Sikh War. Image Courtesy: BritishBattles.com

CHAPTER 14

THE ANGLO-SIKH WARS

1845 AND 1848

The Anglo-Sikh Wars of 1845 and 1848 are the only two examples where the generals betrayed their own army. These wars changed the course of Indian history. Generals Tej Singh and Lal Singh betrayed their own Sikh Army to join hands with the British. In the first Anglo-Sikh War, Governor General Sir Henry Hardinge was ready with 7,000 troops of the British Bengal Army. The entire British Army, which included the soldiers of the East India Company, had five divisions and 13,000-odd troops.

During the first Anglo-Sikh war, the sons of Maharaja Ranjit Singh died one after another. His son, Sher Singh, was shot by his own cousin at point-blank range, while his grandson Nau Nihal Singh was killed while returning from his father's funeral. If the generals had not been disloyal, the Sikhs would not have lost the first war. Amar Pal Sidhu has written an interesting book on the Anglo-Sikh Wars, highlighting the vulnerabilities of the British Army and how close it came to surrendering.

Hardinge was at Ferozshah and preparing to lay down arms. "The British Army had not eaten for days, had not had water for 20 days, and had run out of ammunition. It was frail and incapable of fighting further. If only Generals Tej Singh and Lal

Singh had not betrayed their Sikh army, the British would have surrendered and created a significant moment in the Indian history, which would have changed its course".

The Sikh Empire and the British East India Company fought its first Anglo-Sikh Conflict in 1845 which lasted till 1846. This was fought in and around the Ferozepur district of Punjab. It led to the defeat and partial conquest of the Sikh empire and cession of Jammu and Kashmir as a separate princely state under the British rule. There were mutual demands and indictments against the Sikh Durbar and the East India Company. Frequent attacks on each other caused the diplomatic relations to become insolvent. The Army of East India Company began marching towards Ferozepur. Sir Henry Harding, the British Governor General of Bengal, placed himself below Gough in the military chain of command accompanied Sir Hugh Gough, the Commander-in-Chief of the Bengal Army. The forces of the British East India Company comprised formations of the Bengal Army, with one British unit to every three or four Bengal infantry or cavalry units.

General Raja Lal Singh, who led the Sikh Army, along with Tej Singh, betrayed the Sikhs during the war. The two generals regularly supplied information to the British officers and even received orders from them. The Sikh army crossed the Sutlej on 11 December 1845, in response to the British movement. Although the leaders and most of the army consisted of Sikhs, but there were also a number of Punjabi, Pakhtuns and Kashmiri infantry units. Though the Sikhs claimed that they moved only into Sikh occupied areas (specifically the village of Moran, whose ownership was in dispute), but the British regarded this as hostile and declared war. After Raja Gurdit Singh's death, his son Ajit Singh, succeeded him. To face the British, Ajit Singh upgraded his fort at Ladwa. He fought on the side of the Sikh army, against the British during the First Sikh war in 1845 and faced defeat.

Historians have done a lot of research on the Sikh battles. The second Anglo-Sikh War took place when Multan intimidated and killed two British officers. The army, under General Sher Singh Attariwala, son of General Chattar Singh Attariwala, joined the revolutionaries on the banks of the overflowing Chenab River. A military conflict took place between the Sikh Empire and the British East India Company in 1848-49. This conflict resulted in the fall of the Sikh Empire and the seizure of Punjab which subsequently became the North-West Frontier Province (NWFP), by the East India Company.

On 19 April 1848, Patrick Vans Agnew of the civil services and Lieutenant William Anderson of the Bombay European regiment were assigned to take charge of Multan from Diwan Mulraj. They were both slayed, and shortly the Sikh troops joined the revolt. Lord Dalhousie, the Governor General of India, agreed with Sir Hugh Gough, the Commander-in-Chief that the British East India Company's military forces were not only insufficient but were also inadequately equipped with transport and supplies. They were not prepared to go to the battlefield. Despite the victories gained by Herbert Edwardes against Mulraj, and the indecisive victories that Gough accomplished at the Battle of Ramnagar in November and at the Battle of Chillianwala on 13 January 1849, the resistance at Multan showed that they were still unprepared and needed all the government's resources.

On 22 January 1849, Multan was won over by General Whish, who was all set to join Gough's army. On 21 February, Gough won the Battle of Gujrat. The British then pursued the Sikh Army to Rawalpindi, where it was forced to lay down its arms, after which their Afghan allies retreated from Punjab. After the victory at Gujrat, Lord Dalhousie annexed Punjab for the East India Company in 1849. He received the thanks of the British parliament for his services and a step in the peerage.

To protect undivided India, there are many famous battles by Sikhs that show how they tried guarding the soil, and especially Lahore. The Mughal-Sikh Wars, The Afghan–Sikh Wars, The Gurkha-Sikh War (1809), The Sino-Sikh War (1841-1842), The First Anglo-Sikh War (1845–1846), The Second Anglo-Sikh War (1848–1849) and the dissolving of the Sikh Empire after 1849.

Maharaja Ranjit Singh established the Sikh Empire (1799–1849 CE). It fought many enemies, including the Durrani Empire of Afghanistan and the British East India Company. The Sikhs held their weapons for the first time against the Mughal Empire under Guru Hargobind. His father was the fifth Guru Arjan Dev Ji, and was executed by Jahangir, the Mughal ruler. After his father's death the need for self-defence was felt and Shri Guru Hargobind Singh added the battle-hardened element to Sikhism, which was until then a religion mainly focused on spirituality. He then started recruiting an army. They were called the "Risaldar" wherein, the men were trained in cavalry and Martial Arts. He started using Royal symbols like wearing a "Kalgidhar Turban".

Shri Guru Hargobind Ji asked his followers to bring him gifts of horses and weaponry only. So, at one point the sixth Guru was commanding a cavalry of 700, who fought several battles during the 1620s and 1630s. These battles were mostly against Shahjahan's forces and and some other commanders of Poadh and Majha. In 1699, Guru Gobind Singh, the tenth and last Guru, formed Sikhs into a military sect called Khalsa (which means "pure"), when they fought against the Mughal emperor Aurangzeb. In 1708, before his death the Guru sent Banda Singh Bahadur to lead the Sikhs. Banda Singh Bahadur had excellent combatant skills and managed to weaken the Mughal's control over India. He was captured and beheaded in Delhi in 1716, during the reign of Farrukhsiyar.

Gradually, the Sikhs were organised into Misls. Nadir Shah of Iran attacked India in 1738 and looted Delhi, after which the

Mughals could never recover their power in Punjab. Later, there were constant invasions of Punjab by of Ahmad Shah Durrani of Afghanistan, who was always defeated. Abdali attacked many times but had to return to Pashtun territories ultimately. His final attack of Punjab was in 1767, after which the Sikhs reclaimed Lahore. In 1790, Ranjit Singh of Sukerchakia became Misldar and started uniting all the Misls. He finally took over Lahore in 1799. He was coronated on 12 April 1801 which marks the start of the Sikh Empire. Under his rule the whole of Punjab, Kangra, some parts of Kashmir and for a short while, the city of Peshawar were conquered.

After settlement with the British Government in 1809, Maharaja Ranjit Singh focused on Kangra. The Gurkha General Amar Singh Thapa and Raja Sansar Chand of the Kangra valley had a lot of differences. In the meantime, since Sansar Chand lost hope for his life he sent his brother, Fateh Singh, to the Maharaja for help. In return, the Maharaja asked for the Kangra fort, to which Sansar Chand agreed.

By the end of May, Maharaja reached Kangra with his vast army. All the medieval chiefs were present with their respective militias. There were about ten thousand horses and foot soldiers with the Maharaja, according to Munshi Sohan Lal's estimate. All the hill chiefs were asked to block all passages to stop all means for the Gorkha army to obtain provisions and equipment.

Finding an appropriate time, the Maharaja launched an attack on the Gurkha army and seized their positions about a mile in front of the fort. The Gurkhas fought fearlessly, but still lost the battle. Hereafter the Gurkhas pitched a battle near the Ganesh Valley but the Maharaja sent another army division there. The combat was fierce and blood-spattered. Both sides showed their skills equally. But the Gurkhas had to retreat suddenly due to lack of supplies. Though the Sikhs suffered heavy losses during this war, they won the battle and the Gurkha Army finally surrendered.

Ranjit Singh occupied most of the fertile land of the Kangra valley by 1805, reducing the Katochs of Kangra and the neighbouring rajas to vassals. After the First Anglo-Sikh War of 1846, they ceded the total area to the British East India Company, which eventually integrated into the Punjab province. They assigned the Katochs and the Rajas of the surrounding hills into small jagirs over which they had the rights of revenue and magisterial authority.

In 1813, the Durrani prime minister, Wazir Fateh Khan captured Attock. Punjabi relief force was all set to face them. In the heated summer, Dewan Mokham Chand marched with his army and blocked the Afghans from getting water from the river. Without water, the Afghan troops suffered dehydration, so they attacked multiple times towards the river, but could not break through. Realising that the Afghans were weakening, Mokham Chand attacked Afghans who ran away, losing two thousand men.

The barricade of Multan ended the Afghan influence in Peshawar in 1818. Sikhs took over Peshawar. A fresh battle took place in the Shopian region of Kashmir. This was part of the 1819 Kashmir excursion, which led to Kashmir becoming annexed by the Sikh Empire. The Battle of Peshawar took place on 6 May 1834.

Post-independence it was decided that each Punjabi family would give one son for the cause of Sikhism. Some believe that Sikhism was an extension of the Bhakti movement which is not true. The Bhakti movement was an important historical religious movement of medieval Hinduism that sought to bring religious reforms to all strata of society by adopting devotion to achieve salvation. The movement was prominent in the eighth-century in south India (now Tamil Nadu and Kerala states), and spread northwards. It swept over east and north India from the 15th century onwards, reaching its zenith between the 15th and 17th centuries CE and combated Islam.

Even then the Sikhs played a vital role in this movement. Sikh Guru Teg Bahadur resisted forcible conversion of Kashmiri Pandits to Islam and was beheaded. Sardar Tara Singh demanded a region based on religious identity and went on a fast unto death. The then PM Nehru told him that in a secular India it is extremely improbable to have a state on religious grounds, but he would still 'consider it'. Tara Singh broke his fast and Nehru considered the issue but did not accept it. The Separatist movement for Khalistan was basically funded by Sikhs all over. Thus, the Khalistan movement failed and remained alive only in talk shows and prime times of India and Pakistan. Thousands of Sikhs sacrificed their life for India including Shaheed Bhagat Singh, who fought for an independent India which has equal rights for all. There are several examples of Sikhs standing on Indian soil, but politically motivated entities and media always created a wrong notion about Sikhs as Khalistani extremists and attacked them. Sikhs are one of the strongest clans on the globe, but to disparage them all efforts are made by those who see their existence as a threat.

CHAPTER 15

THE 2020–2021 INDIAN FARMERS' PROTEST

AGAINST THREE FARM ACTS

Media and social media interpreted the agitation of the Punjab farmers against three farm laws as the Khalistan movement to destabilise the Modi Government. Local politicians were rabble-rousing to keep up the tensions, and the Sikhs feared for their lives. The Indian farmers' protest in 2020–2021 was against three farm bills passed by the Parliament of India in September 2020. Farmer unions and opposition politicians said that this would leave farmers at the "mercy of corporates" and described these as "anti-farmer laws".

The farmers demanded a Minimum Support Price (MSP) bill so the corporations would not be able to control the prices. However, the Union Government tried to explain that the laws will help the farmers to effortlessly sell their produce directly to big buyers. The government also stated that the protests were based on misrepresentation. Though India is self-sufficient in the production of food grains and has a number of welfare schemes in place, still hunger and nourishment are serious issues as India ranks as one of the worst countries in the world where food security parameters are concerned.

Soon after the government introduced the bills, there were local protests by farmer unions, mostly in Punjab. After two months of dissent, farmer unions of Punjab and Haryana started a movement called Dili Chalo (Let's go to Delhi), wherein thousands of farmers marched towards the capital city. The law enforcement agencies of various states were asked by the Indian Government to stop the protestors from entering Haryana and from there Delhi.

Water cannons, batons and tear gas were used to do the needful. A nationwide strike was held in November 2020 to support the farmers and thousands gathered at various state borders of Delhi. Between 14 October 2020 and 22 January 2021, eleven rounds of talks took place between the Central Government and the farmers' unions. A section of farmer unions did protest against the bills, but the Indian Government claimed that there were many unions that supported the farm laws. There was a hashtag trending on social media which said that the real farmers were in the fields while Khalistanis were at the border. Media had gone gaga during that period. They called the so-called farmers to the studios announcing the agitators, leftists and Khalistan separatists. Canada and Pakistan funds them to create turbulence in India.

By mid-December 2020, the Supreme Court of India had received a number of petitions seeking the removal of obstructions that had been created by protesters around Delhi. In January 2021, the Apex Court stayed the implementation of the farm laws. Leaders of the farmers and their unions welcomed the stay order, which still remains in effect. On India's Republic Day, 26 January 2021, farmers held a parade with a large convoy of tractors and came to Delhi. Since the protesters veered from the pre-sanctioned routes allowed by the Delhi Police, there was violence and clashes with the police. The protesters then reached Red Fort and put-up farmer union flags and religious flags on the ramparts of the Red Fort.

Punjabi actor-turned-activist Deep Sidhu who died in a road accident near Delhi was accused of violent protest. He hoisted the Nishan Sahib flag on the Red Fort while exercising his democratic right to protest. The flag was light yellow with a 'khanda' printed on it. A 'Khanda' is the emblem used in Sikhism, which contains a double-edged sword, chakra and two single-edged swords. This was introduced in Guru Gobind Singh's era. The Nishan Sahib is a light yellow-coloured flag that is hoisted on every Gurudwara, except those of Nanaksarias. The sixth Guru Hargobind Ji introduced it but that version was without the emblem. Media trials kept calling it a Khalistan flag. The protestors hosted Indian national flag along with Khanda but most of the media debates were hell bent on proving them terrorists and anti-nationals.

On 19 November 2021, the Union Government repealed the bills while on 29 November 2021both houses of Parliament passed the Farm Laws Repeal Bill, 2021. Even after the announcement of the repeal of the farm laws, farmer unions continued with their demand for guaranteed MSPs. They wanted to remind the government of its aim of doubling the farmers' income by 2022. They were again called thankless and deliberate troublemakers.

The Government took too long time to repeal the bills. They tried their best to demoralise the agitation, but the farmers were not in a mood to be appeased or bargain. By 9 January 2021, five farmers had committed suicide. On 16 December 2020, Sant Baba Ram Singh, a Sikh priest, shot himself at the Singhu border. On 18 December 2020, a 22-year-old farmer killed himself by consuming poison in his village after returning from Singhu. On 27 December 2020, Amarjit Singh Rai, a lawyer, committed suicide again by taking poison. Rai left a note which said that he was "sacrificing his life" in solidarity with the farmer's protest and urged Prime Minister Narendra Modi to "listen to the voice of the people".

On 2 January 2021, Kashmir Singh Ladi, a 75-year-old farmer from Bilaspur in Uttar Pradesh ended his life. He was the fourth farmer to do so after 26 November 2020, when the protesters were stopped by the UP Police on the Delhi-UP- Ghazipur Border, which is also known as UP gate. Kashmir Singh, who had been camping at the border since 28 November 2020, along with his son, and grandson, hung himself in a toilet. He too, had left a note in Punjabi that says, "Till when shall we sit here in the cold? This government is not listening at all. Hence, I give up my life so that some solution emerges".

On 9 January 2021, Amrinder Singh, a 40-year-old Punjabi farmer, killed himself by swallowing Aluminium Phosphide tablets at the Singhu border. He had been depressed by the dialogues with the government and downed the tablets at the stage which had been set up for protesters to speak. Though he was rushed to the hospital, but the doctors were unable to save him.

On 30 November 2020, PM Modi expressed his anxieties over the issues of misled and radicalised farmers. Citing that the opposition members have always been spreading lies, Modi said that the old system was not being replaced, instead new options were being put forward for the farmers. The PM wanted to avoid conflicts with farmers ahead of the Uttar Pradesh elections so, he repealed the laws while passing the buck at the opposition.

The UP election results have given one strong message that no matter how much you mess with the government you cannot stop them from coming to power. All those Sikh farmers had to return quietly to their state, and the so-called custodian of the farmer's agitation Rakesh Tikait, failed to change the political discourse.

There was fake news in circulation that a group of Nihangs had claimed responsibility for the brutal murder of a 35-year-old man, at the Singhu border, allegedly because he had disrespected the Sikh Holy book. In April 2020, Nihangs attacked a Punjab Police party in Patiala and chopped off the hand of an Assistant Sub-Inspector when he was stopped for a curfew pass in the midst of the lockdown. Hate crimes and biased incidents are a national problem, but there's no reliable data on the nature or prevalence of the violence.

Many national and international voices came in support of the farmers. Punjabi singers to actors everyone supported the spirit of farmers. Some young environment activists were also attacked and arrested. Film actress, Kangana Ranaut loose cannon, lashed out on social media to attack the farmers and the agitating women. The entire national main stream media was against the farmers. There were prime time debates to demoralise the farmers by calling them terrorists. But no pressure tactics worked. Finally, the Government was forced to take back their Bills and that is how there is some calm.

The State Legislative Assembly general elections in Goa, Manipur, Uttar Pradesh and Punjab are crucial for each political party. No doubt farmers will be playing a crucial role in deciding the fate of the contestants.

CHAPTER 16

SIKHISM

THE WAY OF THE GURUS

There are many arguments and debates about the origin of Sikh religion. Some say their Gurus were Hindus from different parts of India, while others say that as Baba Saheb Ambedkar had founded "Neo Buddhism" to counter discrimination, Guru Nanak ji adapted a faith which was different from Hinduism and Islam. The Sikh religion was started around 1500 CE. Over the next few centuries nine Gurus followed Guru Nanak and established Sikhism.

Five people from different parts of India with different social backgrounds were baptised to Sikhism, to form the Khalsa (ਖ਼ਾਲਸਾ). These first five, then baptised Guru Gobind Singh ji into the Khalsa fold. This is the order of Khalsa, which has a history of around 300 years. The history of Sikhism is associated closely with the history of Punjab in the 17th century. Sikhism clashed with Mughal laws during the reign of the Mughal Emperor Jahangir (r. 1605–1627). The conflicts were due to political progressions of Mughals which were being affected by Sikhism while they valued the Islamic saints. Many prominent Sikhs were killed by the Mughals for not obeying their orders and for opposing the coercion of Sikhs.

The Mughals also cruelly eliminated Guru Arjan Dev and Guru Teg Bahadur along with Banda Bahadur (1716), Bhai Mati Das, Bhai Sati Das and Bhai Dayala and the seven- and nine-year-old sons of Guru Gobind Singh.

To oppose the Mughal domination, Sikhism militarised itself. Religious tolerance and pluralism with Christians, Muslims and Hindus in positions of power branded the rise of the Sikhs under the misls and the Sikh Empire under the reign of Maharajah Ranjit Singh (r. 1792–1839). The peak of Sikhism in the political sphere is the creation of the Sikh Empire in 1799. In those days, many Muslim and Hindu farmers had converted to Sikhism. The Sikh Empire was expanded to the Khyber Pass by Hari Singh Nalwa, the Commander-in-Chief of the Sikh Army along the north-west Frontier during 1825 to 1837. The Sikh Empire's secular administration included innovative military, economic, and governmental reforms.

The preliminary motive of Sikhism was to oppose the forcible conversations. They rose beyond Islam and Hinduism or any other religious bonds, but today, many think tanks establish their ancestry to Hinduism, forgetting the fact that they have already disassociated themselves from religious boundaries. The Sikh Gurus opposed conversions, but today a number of cases of Sikhs getting converted to Christianity are being witnessed in Punjab and across the globe.

Sikh organisations, including the Chief Khalsa Diwan and Shiromani Akali Dal led by Master Tara Singh, strongly opposed the partition of India. Many Sikhs laid their lives to protect India from invaders; they shed their blood for the independence of India. Post-independence, when Gandhi agreed to separate Pakistan, Punjab witnessed a lot of conflict between the Sikhs and Muslims. This resulted in the religious migration of Punjabi Sikhs and Hindus from West Punjab and a similar migration of Punjabi Muslims from East Punjab. Presently, most of the Sikhs live in Punjab in India.

Sikhism was born out of disparagement of evils of rituals, customs and identity politics prevailing among Hindus and Muslims ('Na main Hindu Na Musalman' - Guru Nanak). Now, Sikhism itself is part of the identity politics with its own customs and rituals. It has stopped criticising Hinduism and Islam as it has become too protective about its own tradition. All this has turned Sikhism into just another religion or religious group. Sikhism has lost its way by turning itself into another organised religion. The Sikh community members allowed themselves to fall into the category of vote bank by diluting the prime motive of its existence.

As a religion, I respect it and leave to others to dive into. As a race with a strong reputation of fierce fighters, I have the utmost respect for their traditions. Even during the Mughal rule, Sikh's were much sought after as soldiers and feared by their enemies. In both the World Wars they displayed exceptional bravery not only in the British Army, but everywhere else that they were sent to fight.

Though being a fighting clan, the Sikhs were not called Kshatriyas because Sikhism does not believe in the caste system. Sikhs abolished casteism and give equality to all humans. Sikhism encourages humanity. It teaches a Sikh to serve the human race and facilitate the survival of human life. This is evident at every level of the society, from the langar, a free meal organised by the Sikhs in their Gurudwaras to the national and international level in case of any natural disaster. Gurudwaras never deny access to any human, irrespective of caste and creed. NGOs like Khalsa Aid believe in serving humanity in times of natural disasters. They manage to reach all places of calamities where sometimes even a normal person is unable to do so. During the COVID lockdown, the Sikh community members distributed food, water, oxygen cylinders and even basic masks. They took care of the police working at the check posts. They reached all those places where humans were calling God for help.

Sikhism aims at spreading the philosophy of God as service to mother earth. It aims at preventing hatred in the name of God and promoting peace and harmony among the people of all religions. Above all, Sikhism also preaches that just because you are polite does not mean you are weak. One of the 5Ks of Sikhism (*Kirpaan*) is an excellent example. A Sikh is a soldier saint and if the need arises, a Sikh can prove that he/she is not weak by fighting against wrongdoing. Sikhism encourages learning. The name Sikh itself means 'learner' in Punjabi. It preaches that there is no age for learning and encourages the people to enhance their knowledge.

Sikhs also believe in *'Ik Onkar'* which means that God has one form and it intends to promote religious harmony and prevent fighting based on religion. And to those who say that Sikhism promotes violence by adding the *Kirpaan* to the 5Ks, Sikhism has a long history of violence where many Sikhs were either forced to convert to Islam or beheaded. And yes, Sikhism preaches that "be powerful not to dominate over others, but to conquer and elevate yourself". And to those who make fun of the turban and beard of the Sikh men, it is their religion and they are following it. Every religion in this world has its own unique practice, dress code and life style, which we should respect. And yes, just like a lion is incomplete without his curls, a Sikh is incomplete without his beard. What pains me immensely is that some of the Sikhs do not say a word against those who tortured and killed their Gurus, especially Guru Arjan Dev, Guru Teg Bahadur and Guru Govind Singh and his four *Sahebzades* (sons) because they refused to convert to Islam.

Despite being only around 2 percent of the total Indian population, Sikhs comprise around 20 percent of the Indian Armed Forces. You will never see a Sikh without dignity of labour. From the time their religion was formed in the 15th century, Sikhs have never been ashamed of working hard or doing a job that might seem odd in the eyes of other religions. The respect with which they carry their traditional values, culture and everything associated with their religion or their Gurus without hurting the sentiments of other religions is something that every religion can learn from.

Moreover, their beliefs on values like freedom of speech and to practice religion along with justice and liberty for all and defending civil liberties and protecting the defenceless and their never-ending efforts to safeguard those beliefs or do justice to them should be appreciated at the very least for the sake of humanity.

CHAPTER 17

THE MODERN SIKH

MAY NOT BE GULLIBLE

Many politicians tried playing politics with Sikhs by making it about this party vs that party but overall, what I wanted to say is that cutting across all party lines the "present" attitude of Indians towards Sikhs has borne a massive change. Hence, harassment today, is justified as reaction to the anti-national Khalistanis. If the Police clashes with angry protesters and it is given a religious twist and pronounced as State harassment, then it certainly has to be senseless.

The fact of the matter is that today, Sikhs in India have freedom to practice their beliefs. But there are many attacks on them for adhering to those beliefs under the guise of the Khalsa rule books. They are called terrorists for carrying a *Kripan*, they are called anti-national for standing for their rights, they are conveniently declared Khalistani militants when they agitate against the policies of the ruling Government. There are series of prime-time debates to create a perception about Sikhs that suits the political party whom most of the media supports.

Thanks to social media, at least they have some medium of their own to express their views. Numerous issues are displayed on social media. Participation in politics is the biggest threat to

Sikhism today. This clan shows the sharpest decline in population among all communities in the country.

However, experts doing statistical study of human population and sociologists state that the reason for the falling number of Sikhs in the country is the high rate of migration of Sikhs to foreign lands. After witnessing so much betrayal and rejection, the Sikhs feel secure in foreign lands. The rural landscape in the region is filled with houses constructed by NRIs as they stand out due to their western architectural designs. These are occupied only when the owners visit their homeland during holidays. These houses have all amenities that are common in foreign lands. The general trend is that each immigrant from Punjab pulls along his family members and friends as well to the foreign shores. They work hard as Sikhs believe in dignity of labour. From truck drivers to grocery shop owners to taxi drivers, most of them are Sardars.

Millions of Sikhs have migrated across the globe and play a vital role in the populism of Sikhism. The migration of Sikhs had started during the pre-independence era. It is said that Sikhs have settled in virtually all major countries of the world which includes those in UK, USA, Canada, European countries, Australia, and the Middle East. Hundreds of Hindi movies have been made on these Sikh migrants regarding matrimony and lifestyle. They are a close-knit clan and mostly marry within their community. They also have a good social network. Sikhs believe in living and eating lavishly. Wherever they live it becomes their nation, but India remains their homeland even though it has given them a lot of social challenges.

Conversion of Sikhs is a major issue that is bothering the Sikh community. In 1834, Christianity seeped into the Punjab soil. John Lowry and William Reid were the first missionaries to propagate Jesus Christ in this area. Its initial cliques were urban, literate, and socially assorted. Currently, Punjab has seen a rapid upsurge in the number of Christians. Since it is a relatively new phenomenon in Punjab, the Christians here are mostly converts. Initially, it was the Hindus who were converting, but now, most of them are Sikhs. A fresh wave of mass conversions is happening in Punjab and reportedly thousands have avowed the faith.

The sharp surge in Deras, with each of them having hundreds of thousands of followers, is most noticeable in Punjab. One major reason for the propagation of the Deras is the continued acumen of the Dalits within the Sikhism fold. Although Sikhism was established on the principles of equality, which stated no discrimination because of caste, the divide of the Dalits continues. Most villages have separate Gurdwaras and immolation grounds for the so-called lower castes. Despite the religious reforms, the Deras including the well-known Dera Sacha Sauda have a large number of followers from this strata of society. Most of the Deras do not encourage a change of religion, but the mere fact that people prefer to visit the Deras rather than the Gurdwaras, speaks for itself. Sikh religious leaders opposed these Deras, which has also led to several clashes in the past. The Government and political parties back these Deras for their vote bank. Look at Gurmit Ram Rahim Singh, who is convicted for rape and murder but enjoys Z-plus security. He has a huge number of followers and these votes' matter in Haryana politics.

Another reason for the declining Sikh population in India is the growing trend of showing off among the Punjabis, and Sikhs in particular. The male child (Sikhs have a sex ratio of 933 females per 1,000 males) is preferred due to the high spending, including dowry during marriages. This continuous downslide in the number of Sikhs in Punjab can also have a political fallout.

For Sikhs living abroad – many of whom are in the UK, Canada and US – this is a personal choice, as they have strong cultural and family links to Punjab. The Sikh displacement is often the only way in which Sikhs in India are heard, and they unlikely to stay silent. The Sikh Forum says that about 25,000 Delhi families have completely or partially shifted. All the businessmen who could make alternative arrangements in Punjab have done so. Everyone who has an establishment outside Punjab wonders how long he can continue being safe here.

Shiv Sena chief Bal Thackeray.
Image Courtesy: Pinterest

CHAPTER 18

BAL THACKERAY

THE MAN WHO SHIELDED SIKHS IN 1984

In 1984, Congress was the ruling party in Maharashtra, Vasantdada Patil was the Chief Minister and Shiv Sena the major opposition party. Shiv Sena stood in support of Sikhs and Congress was shocked to see this gesture of the senior Thackeray as it was against their political interest. Through some newspaper articles, Thackeray's backing was propagated as a political compulsion and not as an act of humanity. Bal Thackeray's statement immediately after helped the Sikhs in Mumbai as they felt protected. At that time Bal Thackeray's spontaneous action of opposing the attacks on Sikhs was an important decision for all those Sikh families in Mumbai who might otherwise have faced heavy loss to life and property.

Bal Thackeray supported the Sikhs out of utmost humanity but at the same time he never hesitated to remind them of the consequences if they indulged in violence. When a Sikh protester was gunned down allegedly by a bodyguard of the Dera Sacha Sauda chief, Gurmeet Ram Rahim Singh, Bal Thackeray told them not to create any unrest in the state. Those days a large number of Sikhs were seen wandering around the streets of Mulund wielding swords and attacking innocent people, including women. Train commuters were targeted for no fault of theirs. Several women went to the Shiv Sena Shakha in Mulund and complained to the local leader Prabhakar Shinde. Thackeray published a warning in Samna stating that the Sikhs should ask their elders about the Delhi riots in case they had forgotten about them. He further pointed out that if the anti-Sikh riots did not spread to Mumbai in 1984, it was largely because of the Shiv Sena.

He never tolerated violence against innocent Hindus. One person was killed in a clash between two Sikh sects and thereafter, the violence held the city to ransom for two days. When the Sikh bodies presented their case, the Shiv Sena supremo Thackeray warned them that Shiv Sainiks will not be mute spectators to violence against the innocent. Though Punjab stabilised but the situation in Mumbai was unstable due to the violence unleashed by the Sikhs. Shiv Sena appealed to them to maintain peace but even in adverse situations, no Sikh was hurt by the Shiv Sainiks.

While shielding and dealing with Sikh issues, Bal Thackeray was preoccupied with the Marathi followers' struggles with the Communists, Muslim underworld, and businessmen of South India and Gujarati origins. Sikhs living in Mumbai and in the rest of Maharashtra were neither a problem for the local Marathis nor were Bhindranwale's problems with Indira Gandhi a concern for Thackeray. And even Bhindranwale had nothing to do with Maharashtra and Bal Thackeray. Bhindranwale did visit Mumbai once, but only stayed for a few hours at the Gurudwara at Ramabai Colony and then returned to Punjab when the Mumbai Police came looking for him. Some Indira Gandhi loyalist Congress leaders of Maharashtra did spread a lot of news but that hardly made any sense to Shiv Sainiks or their leader Bal Thackeray.

Bhindranwale was very popular among the Sikh youth of Punjab and Thackeray was also popular among the Hindu youth of Maharashtra. Shiv Sena became popular during the 1980s, the same period that saw Bhindranwale emerging as an undeniable Sikh revolutionary figure. If Bhindranwale benefitted Congress in Punjab by weakening the Akali Dal, Thackeray helped the Congress in Maharashtra by weakening the communist movement which had a strong influence over the trade union in the state. Later, Shiv Sena became a very powerful political force that had legislatures not only in the Maharashtra State Assembly but also in the Central Government led by Bharatiya Janata Party (BJP).

When Thackeray passed away in 2012, he was given state honour, his body was covered with the Indian national flag. Those days Congress-NCP was in power at the Centre and in Maharashtra. Bal Thackeray was loved by all political parties of the state, he actually had no political enemies. He always stood like a protector, the city was safe and calm under his command. Sikhs and Sena have very cordial relations even today.

Portrait of Veer Savarkar.
Image Courtesy: BharataBharati

CHAPTER 19

SAVARKAR

AND SIKHISM

Vinayak Damodar Savarkar, a key leader of Hindu Mahasabha, advocated Hindutva and Hindu religion. He spread Vande Matarm as a national hymn. On 1908 December, Vinayak Damodar Savarkar celebrated the birth anniversary of Guru Gobind Singh, in Caxton Hall, in Westminster. Savarkar asked all Indians to join the celebrations. Savarkar was a brilliant orator. He electrified his audience with his speeches; he moved many hearts towards the freedom struggle of undivided India. Savarkar was a staunch follower of Guru Govind Sahab ji, and adored Sikhism. The warrior spirit of the Sikhs fascinated him.

He did a year-long research at the India Office Library, after which he authored a book titled "The Indian War of Independence of 1857". The Britishers banned the book even before it was published. The book was initially written in Marathi in 1908. The book was smuggled into India but the British authorities failed to trace it and the manuscript reached Paris where it was translated into English under the observation of VVS Aiyar. The English manuscript was also sent to Paris. The book was ultimately printed in Holland and smuggled to India under fake covers. This book not only informed the truth about the national revolution of 1857 but also became a bible for the freedom fighters of India.

The Indian writer Surinder K Singh wrote an article in 1988, titled "Punjab Crisis – Lessons from The Forgotten Past". Savarkar tells a story about communication with a Sikh who identified himself as a non-Hindu. As per Savarkar, the Sikh told him that members of his community would "incur no guilt by killing a Brahmin" as it was a Brahmin cook who had betrayed the sons of Guru Gobind Singh, which led to them being captured and then killed by a Mughal king. After this, the Sikhs developed hate for the Brahmin community. In those days cooking was a Brahmin's job.

Savarkar called the Sikh a "dacoit," or rather a debtor who had looted and killed a money-lending Brahmin. Savarkar introduced a second Sikh to counter the "dacoit", Sikh's argument. He described him as "a gentleman". In Savarkar's story, this "gentleman" Sikh, was standing next to the dacoit Sikh and immediately rebuked the latter by pointing out that many Brahmins had earlier "sheltered the Guru". Savarkar was trying to convince the Sikh that all Brahmins were not bad or betrayed others. Similarly, there are good and bad Sikhs too.

Savarkar then argued that the kith and kin of the Maratha king Shivaji betrayed him. But did Shivaji or nation disown their race and ceased to be Hindus? He further put forth the argument that during a battle with the Mughals, Sikhs had abandoned Guru Gobind Singh. He explained that "It was this cowardice of the Sikhs that forced the Guru to "try a despairing move" which ultimately led a Brahmin to betray the Guru's sons. "Therefore, if for the crime of the latter we cease to be Hindus, then for the crime of the former we ought to cease to be Sikhs too," he stated in his book. With this argument Savarkar reached the conclusion that the Guru's sons were killed because of their own "treachery" and not because of a Brahmin's betrayal.

Further, Savarkar spoke about the Sikh religious symbols that would visually separate them from Hindus. According to him, true Sikhs believed in their Hindu lineage. He wrote, "You cannot pick up a lamb and tie a Kachchha and Kripan on it, to make him a lion!

Savarkar emphasised that if the Guru was able to form a band of martyrs and warriors, he was able do so because the race that had produced him as well as the band could be moulded in this way. He said that as soon as one points at a Sikh who has been true to his Guru, then in effect one is pointing at a Hindu". Savarkar added, "So long as our Sikh brethren are true to Sikhism, they must of necessity continue to be Hindus."

Madhavrao Sadashivrao Golwalkar, was the second Sarsanghchalak of the Rashtriya Swayamsevak Sangh (RSS). He was one of the most influential figures of the RSS and agreed with Savarkar regarding Sikhism. Like Savarkar, he too believed that "the poison of political ambition had stirred the demon of separatism" among Sikhs. Golwalkar added, "Guru Gobind Singh had declared 'a true Sikh is one who has faith in the Vedas and Bhagavad Gita and who worships Rama and Krishna'". The RSS believes that Sikhism is a part of Hinduism. Whereas, the Sikhs always believe that they belong to no other religion and that they are different from Hindus, Muslims and Christians. Many Sikh community members did not like imposing Hinduism on Sikhism. The very purpose of Sikhism was to abolish casteism and religious superstition. Savarkar and RSS tried explaining to the Sikhs that they belonged to Hinduism, but Sikhs refused to accept it.

During the late 1990s, when RSS was still trying to make space for itself in Punjab's politics, the then Chief, K Sudarshan held secret talks with Sikh hardliners of the Damdami Taksal. This was at one time headed by Jarnail Singh Bhindranwale, who endorsed Khalistan. There were news reports in the Tribune which stated that Sudarshan had headed numerous such meetings to discuss the status of those Sikh extremists who had been jailed after Operation Blue Star, in which Bhindranwale and hundreds of others had been killed.

According to The Tribune report, the RSS along with its Sikh wing, the Rashtriya Sikh Sangat had opened dialogue with the Khalistan separatists, after gauging the Sikh psyche and aspirations for a separate state. BJP, the RSS's political wing, was then a coalition partner in the Shiromani Akali Dal Government. It is a Sikh-centric party and controls major Sikh religious bodies. The RSS report embarrassed the Akalis, as they had been promising to release the prisoners for a decade. Through the report, the RSS presented itself as the well-wisher of Sikhs, while embarrassing both—the Sikh hardliners and the Akalis.

The RSS effectively used the situation to build its credibility among the Sikh people. It seems they had taken a page from Savarkar's book, by pitting Sikhs against each other, and portrayed Hindus as their saviours. The representation was too philosophical to be overlooked. Prime Minister Narendra Modi's announcement to repeal the three contentious farm laws was made on the occasion of Guru Nanak Jayanti on 19 November 2020. He made it a point to mention that he had chosen the auspicious occasion for the announcement. It could be a coincidence, but the same day, the Rashtriya Swayamsevak Sangh chief Mohan Bhagwat, had gone to a Gurdwara in Chhattisgarh's Raipur to pay his respect.

In his book, 'Essentials of Hindustan', Savarkar constantly argues that "If any community in India is Hindu beyond cavil or criticism, it is our Sikh brotherhood in Punjab, being almost the autochthonous dwellers of the Sapta Sindhu land and the direct descendants of the Sindhu or Hindu people. The Sikh of today is the Hindu of yesterday, and the Hindu of today may be the

Sikh of tomorrow. The change of a dress, or a custom, or detail of daily life cannot change the blood or the seed, nor can it efface and blot out history itself."

This shows the importance Savarkar ascribed to Sikhs remaining within the Hindu fold. At the time of writing his book, he wanted to create a Hindutva narrative and wanted to include the Sanatanists, Satnamis, Sikhs, Aryas, Anaryas, Marathas and Madrasis, Brahmins and Panchamas ('untouchables') under the Hindutva fold. Thus, Savarkar was more progressive than Gandhi, who stuck to his puritanical views of caste and varna. Savarkar said, "The system of four varnas may disappear when it has served its end or ceases to serve it, but will that make our land a Mlechchhas—a land of foreigners? The Sanyasis, the Arya Samajis, the Sikhs and many others do not recognise the system of the four castes, and yet are they foreigners? God forbid! They are ours by blood, by race, by country, by God. We, Hindus, are all one and a one nation, chiefly because of our common blood: Bharati Santati." In his book, 'Essentials of Hindutva', Savarkar has used the word 'Sikh' over 60 times. This shows the importance of Sikhs for him in his Hindutva project. He encouraged the Sikhs to continue professing their religion and continue fighting for minority rights. He added, "The Sikhs are free to reject any or all superstitions they dislike in the Sanatan Dharma," which included the binding authority of the Vedas. Thereby, Sikhs may cease to be Sanatanis, but they cannot cease to be Hindus. "Sikhs are Hindus in the sense of our definition of Hindutva and not in any religious sense," Savarkar explained.

On Republic Day, news channels incessantly ran images of Nihang Sikhs swinging swords and riding horses, with tickers and titles that called them terrorists or rioters. Along the false characterisation of the Nishan Sahib as a symbol of Khalistan, this served to frame Sikh iconography and identifiers as violent—a tactic often used against Muslims.

Agar na hote Guru Gobind Singh sunati hot sabki…
I am a Hindu, because of Guru Gobind Singh ji!
Every Hindu is a bit of Sikh.

Whatever is written and conveyed through various articles, it's the choice of words by the writer and expressions of VD Savarkar, to which no Sikh reciprocates. Today's Sikh doesn't want to buy these arguments of Hindu origin of Sikhism.

CHAPTER 20

VIRTUAL KHALISTANI COMMUNITIES

BRAINWASHING INDIAN SIKH YOUTH?

Sikhs in all parts of India are already well-rooted and successful in their trades. They rule the hearts of the local Indians, because of their charity and hard work. By learning from the mistakes of the past patrician Indians should stay united. Moreover, topics like Khalistan, Kashmir and Hindu Rashtra are not here to be resolved, they are the political tools and they are here to drive political motives. Neither can India ever become a Hindu Rashtra nor is Punjab ever going to become Khalistan. People need to stop falling for such baits. Secession and partition are no longer acceptable in modern India. It can only lead to perpetual misery and unsolvable conflict like SYRIA.

There are hundreds of online Khalistani communities and a huge number of youngsters are active in these groups. The orthodox, narrow-minded approach of the people demanding separation has a lack of vision. Maximum posts contain violent images hastily put up, hailing Khalistan or demeaning India. These groups are trying to brainwash the youngsters. Most of the "Khalistan" supporters have fake profiles.

The language and conduct of participants seem more like Pakistani users. There is a possibility that Pakistan is trying to create complete anarchy. Even those who are actually from Punjab seem to be blinded with rage. These referendums or petitions will only see a Pakistan like failed state at best, or further bloodshed at worst. There is hardly any progressive country in the world that mixes its religion and politics. Religious extremism and bizarre visions can never achieve any constructive outputs. Such sites are driving the youth's sense of rage and falsehood of religious patriotism. Such conditioned youth get into the trap of drugs, dope and a disillusioned state of mind.

People are having open discussions on social media platforms on how to fulfil the demand for a separate Khalistan. The movement is a way to create divide amongst communities. People involved in these activities, the so-called influencers, are the ones settled in the USA, UK or Canada. The growth and development of Punjab in the past 30 years is a clear example of how the state has advanced and grown in terms of lifestyle, healthcare and other areas. The economy of Punjab is stronger than before and the state also holds a very important position in the Indian agricultural scenario.

All those who are closely associated with the culture and thought process of people living in Punjab, do not want referendum 2020 to come up and disrupt the peace in the state. The aim of the so-called Khalistan activists is to create a divide and they are using social media to spread hatred, which is their underlying agenda. The weird thing is that these fanatics have also started floating images of Khalistan passports and currency to influence people. However, the voter turnout in Punjab, which was more than 60 per cent, showcases the belief of Punjab and its residents in democracy and the present Government. In the mid-1980's, the idea of Khalistan had some support from Sikhs but today, Khalistan is nothing but just a fancy idea.

Today, no sensible or educated Sikh supports Khalistan because it does not make any political, social or economic sense. Sikhs are completely integrated into the diverse multicultural social fabric of India, have sound political representation and are the most affluent community in the country. Today, Indian Sikhs are working for some of the best software companies in the world in Bangalore or Hyderabad or for some of the biggest financial firms in Mumbai or Delhi or have set-up manufacturing plants catering to a market of 1.25 billion people. Media also has a number of Sikh employees with many successful Sikh journalists.

Its high time the fringe elements stopped dreaming about Khalistan, Kashmir, Hindu Rashtra and Tamil Nadu, etc. Sitting in countries across the globe and making decisions for Punjab is not a good idea. None of us want to ever go and live in Khalistan. There is nothing wrong with Punjab being a part of India. Already the Punjabi youth is addicted to drugs, doping and is depressed. Such online communities either brainwash them or leave them dejected. This is another betrayal for the community at large.

India Sikhs are fighting against policy failure, repealing laws, and have a vision for glorious farming. But none of them came on road with unreasonable demands for Khalistan. Sikhs are known for their Nobel works; they are the backbone of social stability. For that matter, no youth should be exploited against one another for criminal hate. Look at Bulli Bai and Sulli deal operators, they are young Indians who have hardly seen the world but are conditioned to attack minorities. Where are we leading this generation? Social media has become fanatical training centres. Instead of asking for some or the other division, ask for absolute unity in the nation. Ask for basic dignity for minorities and open-mindedness in the majorities.

REFERENCES

The author would like to give due credit to the sources for relevant information.

https://www.tribuneindia.com/news/archive/features/sikh-prisoners-ins--outs-of-jail-terms-28539

https://en.wikipedia.org/wiki/First_Anglo-Sikh_War

https://www.indianetzone.com/30/veer_savarkar_indian_freedom_fighter.htm

https://caravanmagazine.in/religion/rss-threat-sikh-assertion-farmer-protests-savarkar-golwalkar

Checking copyright holders and obtaining consent, has not been possible in all cases; any lapses brought to our notice will be improved in future editions.

www.ingramcontent.com/pod-product-compliance
Lightning Source LLC
Chambersburg PA
CBHW070129260726

48658CB00001B/320